Many of us enjoy lifestyles that depend on the vast use of resources, but today's levels of consumption are affecting our health and the health of the planet that supports us. We may live in Britain, but our lives are supported by materials, fuels and food from all around the world. And we don't just *use* precious resources; we *waste* them. I once read that a weed is simply a plant in the wrong place; in the same way, a dustbin of rubbish is simply misplaced resources. Most of what we put in our dustbins is valuable and useful in some way – it seems totally crazy that we are literally throwing our world away!

Jo Budd has worked with the Women's Environmental Network since 1990, including researching and writing for their publication *A Tissue of Lies*. She has studied Women's Studies and Third World Studies at Middlesex University and, more recently, Law at City University. Jo has two children and lives in Sussex.

Beyond the Bin
The Livewire Guide to Reusing and Recycling
Jo Budd

Livewire
from The Women's Press

First published by Livewire Books, The Women's Press Ltd, 2000
A member of the Namara Group
34 Great Sutton Street, London EC1V 0LQ
www.the-womens-press.com

Copyright © Jo Budd 2000

The right of Jo Budd to be identified as the author of this work has been asserted by her in accordance with the Copyright, Designs and Patents Act 1988.

British Library Cataloguing-in-Publication Data
A catalogue record for this book is available from the British Library.

This book is sold subject to the condition that it shall not, by way of trade or otherwise, be lent, re-sold, hired out, or otherwise circulated without the Publisher's prior consent in any form of binding or cover other than that in which it is published and without a similar condition including this condition being imposed on the subsequent purchaser.

ISBN 0 7043 4952 3

Typeset in 12/14pt Bembo by FiSH Ltd, London
Printed and bound in Great Britain by Cox & Wyman,
Reading, Berkshire

This book is for everyone who cares enough to make some waste-saving changes in their lives. However small the changes may appear they all add up and make a difference. I hope you enjoy the book and find it a useful tool for empowerment and positive action.

It is also for Ann Link who works so hard and so positively to make the world a better place, for Nick Cobb for his quiet wisdom and practical support, and for our children Freya Leif and Felix Leif who, like all children, deserve to inherit a healthy planet.

Contents

Acknowledgements		ix
Introduction		1
Chapter 1	Waste	5
Chapter 2	Consuming and Using	46
Chapter 3	Recycling	87
Chapter 4	Working Waste	116
Chapter 5	The Way Ahead	128
50 Tips for Action		157
Resources		162

Acknowledgements

Biggest thanks to Ann Link at WEN for sowing the seeds, and for her vision, wisdom and generosity, without which this book would not have grown.

Thanks to everyone else who has provided help and information in putting this book together, including Mum and Dad for babysitting, Charlotte Cole at The Women's Press, Nick Cobb, Clare Hilyard-Melia, Alice Richardson, Richard Page, Helen Lynn, Karen Smith, Manda Helal, Joanna Rucklidge, Ian Woodhurst, Peter Hudson, Evelyn Fulton, John Clarkson, Kevin Crook, Community Composting Network, Surfers Against Sewage, Marine Conservation Society, Tidy Britain Group, Waste Watch, Friends of the Earth, Richard Boden of Wyecycle, The Body Shop, BioRegional Development Group and many more.

Introduction

Many of us enjoy lifestyles that depend on the vast use of resources, but today's levels of consumption are affecting our health and the health of the planet that supports us. We may live in Britain, but our lives are supported by materials, fuels and food from all around the world. And we don't just *use* precious resources; we *waste* them. I once read that a weed is simply a plant in the wrong place; in the same way, a dustbin of rubbish is simply misplaced resources. Most of what we put in our dustbins is valuable and useful in some way – it seems totally crazy that we are literally throwing our world away!

Historians have named whole eras of human development after the materials that were most important to people at that time, and so we have the Stone Age, Iron Age, Bronze Age etc. Today we make use of such a variety of materials it would be impossible to define our lives in the same way. We are the complex 'Modern World'. Sadly, this point in human civilisation might be better recognised by the way that we *fail* to value materials, rather than the way we value them.

The so-called Modern World emerged as Britain, Europe and the rest of the West began the process of industrialisation in the eighteenth century, and now the system of industrial capitalism dominates the lives of most of the peoples of the world. Industrialisation brought social, economic and cultural upheaval, and rapid and continual change has followed ever since. We severed connections between ourselves and the natural world around us. Where once we lived according to natural resources, changing seasons and patterns of daylight, now our water comes from taps, not streams or rainfall, our electric light bulbs come on when the sunlight dims, our food comes from shops, not our gardens, our waste goes into the dustbin – we don't deal with it.

Technology has brought us enormous benefits, but not without costs. Some of the technological processes that make our lives easier and more enjoyable (let alone those that don't) produce massive pollution and waste. And we are so sold on technology that for each problem it creates, we seem to believe that more technology will offer a solution. But high tech isn't always good technology. Developing appropriate technology and clean technology will allow us to enjoy the benefits of an industrial society without damaging the planet.

For many people, past and present, it's poverty that has forced them to be thrifty and resourceful. Reusing and mending are commonplace where money is short. We've been encouraged by the advertising industry to see high levels of consumption and the use of disposable products as signs of wealth and status, of having enough money not to care. It's important to dissociate resourcefulness from poverty, it's up to everyone to care and take responsibility. We need to care and to be proud of caring.

Beyond the Bin is about changing the way we think about rubbish in order to secure a better future for all on planet Earth. If you want to take the rubbish out of your life for good – read on! Chapter One explains how and why waste is a uniquely human problem – looking at a range of issues, from global warming to sustainable development to discuss the importance of radically changing the way we think about waste. The next three chapters explain waste reducing solutions and ways that you can get involved. Finally, Chapter Five looks forward to a less wasteful future, celebrating some of the many ways that people can, and are, taking positive action to create the future they want.

> Until one is committed, there is hesitancy, a chance to draw back, always ineffectiveness. Concerning all acts of initiative, there is one elementary truth, the ignorance of which kills countless ideas and splendid plans: the moment that one definitely commits oneself then Providence moves too... whatever you can do or dream you can, begin it. Boldness has genius, power and magic in it. Begin it now.
>
> Goethe

Chapter 1

Waste

Natural Cycles

Life on Earth is referred to by some as the web of life. Think of a spider's web; its circular shape, its many delicate and connected strands of thread, its usefulness and its beauty. The web has many parts but it is a whole in itself – just like the world, which is a single sphere but is made up of many connected elements that all play a vital role in the workings of the planet.

Planet Earth has been around for over four billion years, although its life hasn't always been the complicated and awesome arrangement of relationships that it is now. Bacteria, plants, creatures, soil, water, weather systems and patterns of day and night are all integrated. Over millions of years plant and animal life has developed and changed. Processes and cycles have evolved and life on Earth has survived and developed by continually adapting to them. Being adaptable is the key to survival.

Nature is also extremely efficient and resourceful. All living things – plants, animals and birds alike – follow a pattern of a) generation, b) life and c) degeneration. Nothing is wasted and all is useful. Even the physical world (for example, rocks and water), which most of us don't consider to be alive, continually cycles – although some of these changes take place on a geological timescale rather than a human one. For example, rocks are often formed from shellfish in the sea. They compact and harden, becoming land, and then are worn away to sand and washed back into the sea where they may eventually be compressed to become sedimentary rock.

Life Cycles

The simplest and most numerous life forms are bacteria. Bugs are everywhere! But don't be deceived by those bleach adverts that would have you wipe out all known germs. Bugs are extremely important and most of them work to our benefit rather than our detriment. In the soil, bacteria and other decomposers, like worms, are major recyclers that play an important role in the web of life.

The decomposers have a role in both degeneration and regeneration. They break down dead plants, leaves, animals and faeces and allow the nutrients contained within them to be released and used over again. Earthworms are particularly valuable decomposers because their burrows also aerate the soil and provide drainage. When organic matter is broken down the rotted matter conditions the soil, giving it structure and the nutrients required for plant life to flourish. This is the natural process of composting.

So vegetation goes through cycles, but, if it weren't for the sun and the miracle that is photosynthesis, there would be no vegetation. Green plants are the first link in all food chains, producing food as if out of nothing. Nutritious soil, water, carbon dioxide from the air and sunlight are the magic ingredients. Their presence is often so familiar to us that they become invisible. We do not see them, but if we underestimate or forget their importance, we do so at our peril, because they are our life support system.

Green plants feed the vegetarians (primary consumers), who in turn provide breakfast, lunch and dinner for the carnivorous or omnivorous secondary consumers. As the links of a food chain are established, the populations at each level tend to decrease so that relatively few creatures occupy the 'top position'. Typical top consumers are birds of prey and large mammals and reptiles. Food chains tend not to exist in isolation in any one habitat so it's more accurate to describe them as food webs because they overlap and to some degree are interchangeable.

Food webs are not static – there can be booms or crashes of populations – but recent research indicates that it is impossible to recreate an ecosystem once it has been destroyed. Even adding all the species in the right order doesn't work. It has to be left to natural processes to build a new system, and this is a long, slow process.

Animals, like plants, are reprocessed when they die. They will be something's idea of a tasty dinner. A successful predator or scavenger will consume the feast and subsequently rearrange its atoms and produce manure. This in turn will keep the insects and bugs busy, and here we are back with composting again! You can see how nature works on the basis of circular movements. Bacteria, plants and animals are all involved in a continuous sustainable process in which waste never occurs because there is never an end product – instead a resource to be used in the next stage of the cycle. One life form's trash is another life form's treasure!

Carbon is one of the building blocks of all life. Living plants absorb carbon dioxide (CO_2) and decaying ones release it so it is available again. Thus the amount of carbon dioxide in the air stays fairly constant. Carbon from past geological ages has been stored in fossil-fuel deposits. When peat, coal, oil and gas are burned to meet our increasing energy demands, we are releasing extra CO_2 beyond that produced by present day vegetation. The burning of fossil fuels has also polluted the water cycle.

In Britain we have largely destroyed our forests, using them for shipbuilding and fuel for iron-making in the

---

Acid rain

Acidification is primarily caused by emissions of nitrogen oxide and sulphur dioxide when fossil fuels are burned. The high temperature of burning makes nitrogen combine with oxygen in the air to form nitrogen oxides, and sulphur compounds in the fuel give sulphur dioxide. The polluting particles are carried long distances by winds and then come down in rain, mist or snow. Acid deposits damage plant and animal life on land and in water. Human water supplies are also threatened by toxic metals which leach out of acidified soil and into groundwater, or out of corroding drinking-water pipes in acidic water areas.

early stages of the industrial revolution. But the forests and other healthy ecosystems in the rest of the world have protected us and kept our climate stable. Now, as the rest of the world industrialises, the whole world could lose this stabilising influence and it will be increasingly difficult for humans to be sustained on earth.

The plight of ancient rainforests that are being destroyed has been one of the prominent campaigns of the environmental movement in recent years. Locally, deforestation has social, economic and environmental consequences – indigenous forest peoples have homes, livelihood and spirituality swept away. The loss of plant and animal species reduces the land's biological diversity, and makes it more vulnerable to ecological disaster. Much of the life in the rainforests has yet to be documented and classified; we have little idea of the value of what we are losing.

Some of the impact of deforestation will be felt on a global level. Ancient forests act as carbon sinks, absorbing much of the excess CO_2 that humans produce, but we are rapidly pulling the plug out of these sinks, taxing the Earth's ability to regulate climate. And much of the carbon that is already locked in the trees will be freed. This deals a double blow to a planet already threatened by global warming (or climate change) brought on by a build up of greenhouse gases.

The greenhouse effect
The major greenhouse gases are carbon dioxide, methane and CFCs. These gases build up in the atmosphere and form a screen which prevents some of

> the radiation from the sun from escaping after it has beamed down. The trapped rays warm the environment – this is the greenhouse effect. The carbon cycle regulates the amount of such gases in the atmosphere but increased production of them through human activities could be tipping the balance. Our ecological equilibrium could be in danger.
>
> The greenhouse effect is a fact. What is less certain is whether an intensified greenhouse effect will result in global warming. Many people feel that we are already experiencing it. Some scientists predict that if we continue to churn out greenhouse gases, then global temperature will rise, ice caps will melt and sea levels will rise. The impact on human life could be dramatic. Ironically, this could make Britain and Northern Europe colder because the changes could impact on the Gulf Stream, which brings warm sea water to the west of the British Isles.
>
> The major contribution to the greenhouse effect comes from CO_2 released by burning fossil fuels. Methane contributes less but it has a more potent effect. Rice paddies, cows' flatulence, landfill sites and coal-mines all produce methane.

Patterns of rainfall will be disrupted because rainclouds previously supplied with moisture from transpiring plants of the forest will be disconnected from this supply. Paradoxically, deforestation can both reduce rainfall and promote flooding. Forests prevent flooding because trees and undergrowth soak up water and release it in manageable amounts that feed steady streams. When roots are destroyed rain runs off quickly, streams become floods, and precious soil chokes rivers and causes more flooding. There will be less rain if the forests have gone, but when it does come, it will do great damage and much of it will be wasted.

When looking at our systems and cycles of life we also see the things that can go wrong when they are upset by human activities. It can be difficult to separate the two. We need functioning cycles to maintain ecological stability. The modern environmental movement was born out of a determination to protect the integrity of our ecology from people's struggle to conquer and improve upon nature. Rachel Carson wrote a book called *Silent Spring* and on its publication in 1962 she was responsible for opening millions of eyes to the devastation being caused by the widespread use of chemical pesticides.

Carson focused on DDT, a synthetic organochlorine pesticide with long lasting and wide ranging effects, that was used increasingly through the 1950s. Its behaviour is typical of organochlorine chemicals. It is stable and so

Rachel Carson

Rachel Carson was an American marine biologist. *Silent Spring* was published just two years before her death from cancer. It was her fourth book and something of a departure from her previous writings, which were about the sea. An impassioned, yet scientific book, *Silent Spring* is still significant today. This is indicated by the fact that nearly 40 years after its first publication it is still in print – and available at your local bookshop!

Carson was probably the first person to warn that the indiscriminate use of chemical pesticides was dangerous to wildlife and humanity through its accumulation in the food chain. She explained the interconnected nature of life, and emphasised that scientific and technological progress doesn't happen in isolation from the wider world.

The book provoked worldwide concern for the environment. The industrial world was forced to begin reconsidering the path it was travelling and the environmental movement began to emerge.

not easily broken down in the environment, and it is fat seeking so it will be stored in the body fat of any creature ingesting it. It is excreted very slowly so amounts stored in the body magnify towards the top of the food chain, and the whole web of life is affected.

In the United States DDT was used to spray Dutch elms and the effects were devastating. Earthworms ate the sprayed leaves and built up DDT in their bodies, and the worms in turn were eaten by robins. Over a four-year period more than a thousand dead birds were reported to ornithologists at Michigan State University. DDT is now banned or restricted in many countries, but in others it continues to be used.

By tracing the movement of DDT through the environment Carson illuminated the cycles within which we exist. Wildlife (notably birds) were affected in two ways. Some were subject to such high concentrations of DDT that had accumulated that they simply died of high dose (acute) poisoning. Others suffered more subtle effects on their reproductive capacity from lower, long term doses (chronic poisoning). This might cause infertility or the production of eggs with thinner shells that are too fragile or do not hatch.

The persistence of this chemical means that it has been found far away from industrial society in places such as Antarctica. It also means that most of us have DDT (along with numerous other persistent chemicals) stored in our body fat. In a startling and poetic way, Rachel Carson reminded us that whatever scientific and technological advances we make, we are still part of nature.

In spite of this, we often behave as if we are separate from nature and the amount of stuff we waste is one way that this is demonstrated. Now, to discuss waste as an environmental issue in the same context as the giant international campaigns of the environmental movement such as deforestation and global warming may seem odd. Waste doesn't sound dangerous or strange – it's a word we are all too familiar with and, to be honest, most of us probably find the thought of it utterly boring. But waste is neither boring nor insignificant. In fact, waste is one of the key themes that unites the broad spectrum that is the environmental movement. An activity or project that is sustainable will not produce waste (though it may create a useful by-product). The amount of waste we produce is like a barometer that measures how sustainable our lifestyles are. Waste concerns may not have the glamorous appeal of cute animals whose habitat is threatened by deforestation, but the issues are every bit as important and, because it's in our kitchen, bathroom etc, much easier to do something about.

Waste is a Human Invention

Waste doesn't occur naturally. Nature continually creates and then uses the by-products of different processes. But as a general rule humans don't. Waste is a human invention because we alone make things that don't transform themselves by rotting or being eaten. We have tended to create linear, rather than circular, processes for the things that we make, and consequently a big pile of rubbish at the end of the line.

Take televisions as an example. Television technology has developed dramatically over the past fifty years. Designs have changed, quality has improved and prices have fallen to the point where virtually everybody has access to a television if they want it. But what about all the broken or simply outdated sets? Some of them get mended but eventually they all reach the end of their days. I would like to say that they all 'meet their maker' and are returned for re-manufacturing but we haven't created a system for this. Lying buried in who knows how many landfill sites across the country are fifty years worth of television sets.

In theory, waste is stuff that is no longer useful, is worn out, not repairable and generally redundant. But sometimes we actually turn useful items into rubbish simply by putting them into the bin – we don't appreciate that there is any life left in them. For many of us a simple change in attitude could dramatically reduce the size of our rubbish bin.

Archaeologists study the human past by analysing the material remains. We think of archaeological digs uncovering bricks, pottery, bones, coins and metal implements. These items help us to recreate a picture of life in the past. I wonder what the average landfill site would look like to archaeologists in 500 or a 1000 years time? Surely it'll appear strange that we have thrown away so much that is valuable?

Think about your own rubbish bin and the things that you throw away. What about the rest of your family or household? And your neighbours? How much rubbish does your town or village collectively create? How many black sacks or wheelie bins are filled up every week and collected by the council? Can you imagine how much space they might take up? And where do they put them? And what would happen if they didn't get taken away, how long would it be before we were buried in rubbish?

The answer is – not long at all. Every year the waste we make in the UK would cover a medium sized city (about the size of Edinburgh) one metre deep. Hold that thought and think twice about what you put in your bin!

I'm sure one of the reasons that we create so much waste is that we don't really have to take responsibility for it. It is the responsibility of each local authority to arrange for the regular collection of household waste free of charge although collection and disposal is paid for with revenue from the council tax. We just put it in the designated container and someone comes by to take it away. In the UK 28 million tonnes of rubbish is collected this way every year.

This is just the post-consumer waste – the rubbish that comes out of our homes from goods that we have bought and used. It doesn't include the pre-consumer waste created by all the activities that support our lifestyles. Power generation, mining, industry, agriculture and commerce each contribute to a yearly rubbish heap that exceeds 430 million tonnes of solid waste. Of course this figure doesn't include the waste created in the production of goods that are imported from other countries. So, huge as they are, these figures do not reflect the full amount of waste created by the demands of modern Britain.

Organising our Rubbish

A huge industry and bureaucracy has grown up to deal with waste. In Britain we are bound by law made by the European Union as well as that made by our national government at Westminster. The EU makes regulations and directives – we are directly bound by regulations but directives set out common aims and deadlines which each national government must then incorporate into their national legislation.

The European Union has a commitment to environmental protection. The European Community Strategy for Waste Management sets out a number of principles to which member countries should adhere:

- the establishment of a 'waste hierarchy' which prioritises how we should deal with waste – prevention is top of the list, followed by reuse, recycling, energy recovery and only then disposal
- the 'proximity principle' which requires waste to be dealt with as close to its source as possible
- the 'producer responsibility principle' which requires those who produce waste to take responsibility for it
- targets for waste reduction and waste recovery.

The present government has published its waste-management plan – 'Waste Strategy 2000'. This sets out a commitment to reduce the amount of waste we produce as a society by a variety of means. The document acknowledges the importance of reducing and reusing, though puts particular emphasis on recycling – for the first time setting mandatory targets. The new strategy means that some local authorities must work hard to improve on the present 9 per cent average rate of recycling, to reach the following targets:

- recycle or compost 25 per cent of household waste by 2005
- recycle or compost 30 per cent of household waste by 2010
- recycle or compost 33 per cent of household waste by 2015.

A few far-sighted councils have long since met the 25 per cent rate. Now it's time for the rest to catch up. The government also intends to set a good example with a procurement policy that ensures government departments buy recycled goods where appropriate – starting with paper. You can find out more about government action on waste by visiting the Department of the Environment, Transport and Regions (DETR) website (address in Resources).

Although local councils have long had a duty to take away rubbish, until recently they had no powers to do anything about the amounts of waste produced in their areas even though waste disposal is getting more difficult and expensive. Local authorities are elected and partly paid for by the people in local areas of the country, but they are restricted to powers given them by national government. Any changes of their powers and duties must come from an Act of Parliament.

The Women's Environmental Network (WEN) found it illogical that local authorities lacked the power to take measures to minimise waste despite the fact that reducing waste is top of the theoretical waste hierarchy. For this reason WEN initiated the Waste Minimisation Bill in 1995, which became law in November 1998.

Under this new legislation local authorities can now:

- include waste minimisation strategies within any waste plan
- give people information about alternatives to wasteful products
- promote laundry services (these avoid waste when washable items replace disposable ones)

- have reduction targets, as well as recycling targets, in waste contracts
- start repair schemes for household appliances which can provide local employment and training
- make alliances with businesses which provide services to avoid wasteful products
- attract companies with positive environmental policies into their area.

The Problem as it Appears

We are surrounded by waste in many shapes and forms. We observe dustbin collections each week and probably witness litter every day. Some of us live close to incinerators, landfills or even Sellafield – Britain's factory for reprocessing nuclear waste. Whether rubbish is being dealt with in an organised way or not, it always represents a blot on the landscape.

Litter

Littering is antisocial, it makes our environment ugly and often poses a danger to wildlife. But did you know it's also illegal under the Environmental Protection Act 1990? Local councils also have the power to appoint litter wardens to patrol and issue £25 fines to litterers – I don't know if any of them are exercising this power – I've certainly never seen a litter warden.

One of the major sources of litter is packaging, especially food and drink containers. Although (under the European Union Directive on Packaging and Packaging Waste) the UK aims to recycle 58 per cent of its 8 million tonnes of packaging waste by the year 2001, this is unlikely by itself to make litter a thing of the past.

If litter doesn't get cleared up it can hang around for an awfully long time. The Tidy Britain Group has made some estimates as to how long it takes different things to degrade in the environment:

- plastic bottles – indefinitely
- aluminium cans – 80–100 years
- tin cans – 50 years
- plastic bags – 10–20 years
- cigarette butts – up to 2 years
- orange peel/banana skin – up to 2 years.

Preventative measures

Even though we have reasonably accessible recycling facilities in Britain we still discard a lot of litter that actually is recyclable. It needs to be easier to recycle the waste we generate. Public litter bins with separate compartments for recyclables are one example of a design solution. Some local authorities already have bins with compartments for cans. Imagine the example it would set if every public bin was a mini recycling centre! You could contact your local council recycling officer and ask whether the council has considered this as a design option next time they replace their bins.

A lot of litter from the fast food industry is plastic, paper and card that is contaminated with food, so it isn't suitable for recycling. Making greater use of reusable cups, plates and utensils and minimising the use of single portion sachets of sugar, salt, vinegar etc would reduce waste and litter *and* work out cheaper in the long run. You may appear a little eccentric taking your own container to a takeaway food shop, or mug to a canteen that uses disposable cups, but that would be an excellent way of getting your point across while saving waste and litter and hopefully encouraging others to do the same. And anyway, is there anyone who actually enjoys drinking out of plastic cups?

On the beaches
Litter is a problem on our beaches too. It creates a hazardous and unpleasant environment for wildlife and humans alike. Every September, the Marine Conservation Society organises a campaign called Beachwatch which involves teams of volunteers not only clearing up litter from our beaches but also recording what type of litter and how much of it was found.

The statistical information is valuable because the major sources of the litter can be identified. The Marine Conservation Society has used the results of their surveys to urge the government to place better controls on the disposal of waste at sea and on land, and to inform and encourage everybody to take responsibility for the wellbeing of our environment.

If you want to get involved with a Beachwatch survey then contact the Marine Conservation Society (see Resources).

> ### Beachwatch 1999 facts
> Bad weather over the Beachwatch weekend meant that fewer volunteers surveyed less beaches than in previous years. But these are the facts! 171 beaches were cleaned and surveyed by over 1600 volunteers. 11,618 kg of litter was recovered from approximately 92 km of coastline. Four main sources of litter on the UK coastline were identified: tourist and recreational litter (38.6 per cent),

> shipping waste (2.6 per cent), sewage related debris (13.5 per cent) and discarded fishing gear (11.2 per cent). Plastic items represented over 50 per cent of all debris recorded, as they have done since Beachwatch started in 1993. Cotton-bud sticks remained in the top ten most common items.

Bag It and Bin It

Bag It and Bin It is a national campaign that was launched in 1995 and is supported by many organisations (including the Women's Environmental Network – check out their sanitary-towel disposal bags!). Its aim is to encourage people to stop using the toilet as a dustbin and start bagging and binning items that were previously flushed away. Its major focus is on sanitary products, which for decades we have been encouraged by manufacturers to flush away out of sight (and out of mind).

About one third of Britain's sewage is discharged to sea, with little or no treatment. Much of what we flush away enters the sea and is washed up on the beaches later. This includes sanitary towels, tampons, condoms, cotton buds, even syringes – not to mention bacteria and viruses. When sewage is treated inland the bits of debris are screened out and then have to be disposed of. This makes water treatment more complicated and expensive than it needs to be. Flushing our bathroom waste away is not a suitable disposal option, it simply moves the problem along. Sewage can be digested by microbes to make useful, harmless fertiliser (but not if it's mixed with plastic litter or poisonous chemicals). Anything else that gets flushed down the toilet can create litter which is unsightly and potentially dangerous for all users of the beach environment.

Surfers Against Sewage also support Bag It and Bin It. Since 1990 they have campaigned against sewage disposal and toxic dumping at sea. Their campaign has grown and gained momentum and is a great example of how a small group of people with a purpose can really begin to change things. Contact them for more information about what they do and details of their groovy merchandise! (See Resources.)

Authorised disposal of waste

For wastes that do not enter the sewage system, the main disposal options in Britain are burying or burning (incineration). The majority of waste goes directly to landfill. Only a small percentage is incinerated and even then the remaining ash is landfilled. Both methods have associated environmental problems which give us even more reason to reduce the amount of waste we create. We all know that these problems exist. Proposals for new landfills or incinerators are never welcomed by local people who will be affected by such development.

'Nimby' stands for 'not in my back yard'. In the past many local protest groups have said 'not in my back yard' to a variety of schemes which threaten the environment. The term 'nimby' is often used with some derision to describe people who don't want changes on their doorstep. It is implied that these people simply want the scheme or development to take place elsewhere. Many protesters now use the slogan 'not in anybody's back yard'. This better reflects the wide ranging concern that many environmental protesters feel.

Local actions may grow out of local environmental concern but they can also be a trigger for wider environmental consciousness. If the right connections are made we can see and understand the relationship between protesting against an incinerator and avoiding over-packaged goods. If we don't make so much rubbish we won't need to threaten the environment by disposing of it.

Landfill

Each country or region of the world has developed particular ways of dealing with waste depending on local circumstances. Although waste in Victorian towns was often burned, for most of the twentieth century Britain buried its waste in holes in the ground (82 per cent of household waste is landfilled). This practice developed as a result of Britain's geology. This island is rich in many useful minerals and for hundreds of years we have been mining and quarrying out these minerals and leaving holes in the countryside. Rather than spending money on restoring the land to some kind of normality, mineral companies can turn the space into a rubbish dump.

Landfill has been Britain's cheapest and easiest waste-disposal option. In the past landfills have been poorly regulated and serious problems have resulted. Controls are now tighter – since 1996 the Landfill Tax has served as a financial incentive for local authorities to reduce the waste that they send to landfill. The tax is levied on each tonne of waste taken to landfill so it is in the interests of each local authority to maximise recycling and composting, and to support all waste minimisation-projects. But there is still cause for concern and room for improvement.

The ecological threat of landfill begins with the production of methane. When organic matter such as kitchen and garden waste, and even paper, decomposes underground without air, methane is produced as a by-product. Methane is a flammable gas and a valuable fuel. When it is allowed to accumulate the gas represents a safety hazard, an explosion waiting to happen. When it escapes it contributes to the greenhouse effect; in this respect it is 30 times more potent than carbon dioxide.

Within the European Union 32 per cent of methane produced comes from landfills. The EU Landfill Directive aims to tackle this problem by reducing the amount of organic waste disposed of this way. Our government has set the following targets to reduce biodegradable household waste:

- 75 per cent of 1995 levels by 2010
- 50 per cent of 1995 levels by 2013
- 35 per cent of 1995 levels by 2020.

If we all get used to separating our organic waste at home there is massive potential to develop home and community composting. However, there is a concern that where waste does not get separated at source it will end up being incinerated because of the landfill restrictions.

Another by-product of organic decomposition is a liquid known as leachate. The mixture of waste in landfills means that invariably this liquid contains toxic substances. Batteries containing heavy metals which are thrown in the dustbin and end up in landfills will leak out these poisonous metals and contribute to toxic leachate. Escaping leachate is likely to contaminate groundwater – our underground supplies of drinking water. (Most batteries should be placed in the hazardous household waste containers at a household waste site. The only batteries that can be recycled at the moment are from watches and some calculators and cameras – the jeweller will usually accept these back for recycling because of their valuable silver content.)

While in use, landfills degrade the environment by being ugly and smelly while large lorries carrying rubbish to the site increase traffic pollution. Landfills also limit the options for future use of the land since it may become precarious and give way as the rubbish slowly decays. And who would want to live, work or play above an accident waiting to happen?

Incineration

About 6 per cent of Britain's household waste is burned in incinerators, usually with energy recovery. In the 1960s, as the amount of waste increased, large incinerators, based on coal furnace designs, were built by some local authorities. It was a tempting solution because it seemed that virtually all of the waste could be mixed together and destroyed to leave an inert ash. Most people believed fire to be a cleansing process but in fact, although high temperatures destroy microbes, they leave toxic metals like lead and mercury unchanged.

> ### Dioxins
> Incineration can also create new persistent toxic chemicals. Burning mixed waste with synthetic chemicals containing chlorine will create persistent organo-chlorines

> (like dioxins) in the process. Dioxins are a group of chemicals mostly produced as accidental by-products of human activity. They have the dubious distinction of including in their ranks some of the most toxic substances known to humankind. One drop of the lethal 2,3,7,8-TCDD in the equivalent of an Olympic-sized swimming pool would be sufficient to kill fish.
>
> Agent Orange, the defoliant used by the United States in the Vietnam War, was hugely contaminated with dioxins. Vast areas of forest were killed off, but the impact went further. It didn't take long for the Vietnamese people to experience the horrific side effects of the 'defoliant'. Women in particular suffered as they miscarried pregnancies and bore children unimaginably damaged as a result of the poison. Over 30 years later, birth defects are still said to be occurring.
>
> Incineration is a significant source of dioxin creation in the UK.

One or two of the worst 1960s incinerators were quietly shut down after local allegations of effects on health. All are now recognised to have produced large quantities of dioxins. No one is certain because analysis and controls were less accurate in the past, but it is likely that the largest contribution to the dioxins in human body fat has been municipal incineration. The US Environmental Protection Agency has stated that, at the levels present in people in industrialised countries, subtle effects on infant intelligence, on hormones and on the immune system are likely. We get these chemicals through our food, especially animal-fat foods such as dairy products. Dioxins from chimneys fall on grass. Cows eat the grass and cannot excrete the dioxins except in the fat of their milk, which is then drunk by us (unless you're vegan).

This is another example of chemicals like DDT accumulating in the food chain. No one could have predicted in the 1960s that chemicals from burning rubbish could get into our body fat and even into babies before birth, but it happened. Levels are now decreasing, as the old incinerators have been closed down or drastically modified.

However, problems with incinerators are not over. Burning still produces toxic chemicals. High temperatures reduce dioxin formation but produce more nitrogen oxides (which contribute to acid rain). Better arrangements to clean the gases from burning and catch smoke particles mean that the ash is more toxic, and it adds to the cost. Mercury, for example, is a highly toxic liquid metal. It can cause serious damage to the nervous system. For a metal, it evaporates easily, and is difficult to catch amid high volumes of hot gases. Extra devices have to be added to deal with it, with less certainty of success over years of operation. Burning huge quantities of waste and trying to clean the smoke doesn't really make sense!

Modifications to incinerators make them increasingly expensive and the companies that build them need contracts guaranteeing a steady supply of waste to ensure they are financially viable, so they pressurise local authorities to sign up for 20 years or more for a certain amount of waste. This is in direct conflict with aims to reduce waste and conserve resources. Apart from not being a healthy option, incineration isn't flexible enough to promote or adapt to waste minimisation.

Today incinerators usually use the heat from burning to produce steam to generate electricity, like a power station. Operators are dependent on a subsidy (the Non

Fossil Fuel Levy which is taken from our electricity bills) in order to be financially viable – otherwise they would be too expensive for local authorities to afford. So people who object to incinerators are being forced to pay extra for them through household fuel charges! It's not a very efficient way of producing energy as about 70 per cent is wasted, although this can be improved by diverting the hot water left over from creating electricity to heat homes in the local community. This is called 'combined heat and power' – however, not all incinerators that aim to supply heat actually do so. We really need to sort out our values and recycle the recyclables and concentrate increasingly on renewable energy sources to provide heat and power instead of burning up our raw materials.

Recovering heat energy from waste is often presented as equivalent to recycling, but it means that, at best, perhaps half of the bare energy content of a product is recovered. Consider the example of a wooden chair: made from trees, manufactured using human and machine power and no doubt further resources to paint or varnish. The energy needed to make the product cannot be regained, and the damage done by extracting fuels or cutting down forests is ignored.

Nuclear waste

We've looked at waste in fairly general terms up to now but nuclear waste requires a special mention. Nuclear power represents the epitome of unsustainable technology. Fifty years ago the risks associated with nuclear power stations were said to be outweighed by the benefits. The public was told that electricity would be too cheap to meter. Fifty years on the benefits haven't materialised and we are simply left with the fall out. The legacy of nuclear power is dangerous and ugly – a planet polluted with radiation and an accumulation of radioactive waste, spent reactor fuel and redundant nuclear structures.

The contaminated waste holds risks of cancers and genetic defects for contemporary society which doesn't diminish for many generations to come. Future generations have a poisoned inheritance.

Radioactive waste is caused initially when uranium (the main fuel used for nuclear power stations) is mined. Uranium is found in the ground in India, Australia and South Africa where contaminated liquids and solids become a hazard to miners and local environments during extraction. Then, during the production of nuclear power, radioactive gases and liquids are discharged into air and sea, and solid wastes are produced. Plutonium is a man-made element which would not otherwise exist on Earth, formed in nuclear power stations and other reactors. It is radioactive and has a half life of 24,000 years. That means in 240,000 years, one tenth of the plutonium that we have produced in just the last fifty years, will still be here. When you think that humans have only been around for 150,000 years it seems shocking that we have the arrogance to condemn the planet to such a long future of pollution.

What do we do with solids contaminated with radio-activity? In the past they have been dumped at sea, but this has now been suspended by international agreement. The remaining options are storage and shallow or deep burial. Whatever option is used, none of them are safe.

In the not-so-distant past, British Nuclear Fuels (BNFL) were advertising their Sellafield Reprocessing plant as an environmentally friendly recycling operation. The facts are somewhat different. Reprocessing spent fuel from nuclear power stations concentrates the radioactivity and creates the most hazardous types of waste, which are extremely difficult to deal with. Radioactive waste imported from other countries for reprocessing increases the total quantity of Britain's waste and contributes to the fact that Sellafield is the largest single source of civil radioactive discharges in Europe. On top of this, recent revelations have exposed shocking safety standards which make a bad situation worse.

There is no safe way to deal with radioactive waste so we have to stop producing it. There is no justification for continuing with nuclear power when we have safer, cleaner and cheaper ways of producing electricity. I would be relieved to see all the nuclear power stations decommissioned and replaced with wind farms or wave power.

Waste in space

We humans have even managed to litter the space around Earth. Over the past thirty years vast financial resources have been devoted to space exploration. The main contenders in the space race have been the USA and Russia, although Europe, Japan and China have space programmes too. Rockets, shuttles, probes and space stations have all contributed to the assortment of debris that orbits the Earth.

Commercial satellites owned by telecommunications companies also orbit the Earth, supporting our lifestyles, supplying us with television and telephone links right round the world. Inactive satellites are a major contributor to the total mass of space rubbish.

Space debris is a concern because it may collide with working satellites or space vehicles. Such collisions take place at high impact and can cause considerable damage. Such waste may also re-enter the atmosphere and fall to Earth. This could be dangerous, depending on the size of the debris and location of the impact. In addition, our littering of space demonstrates that our lack of regard for the environment extends beyond our world. It's a poor example of human caretaking.

What are We Really Throwing Away?

When we persist in being inefficient and careless in our pursuit of material well-being we are creating a paradox. In our struggle to improve our quality of life we are in fact diminishing it. We are also diminishing the quality of life for other people, plants and animals. The ethic of resourcefulness is usually driven by a concern to preserve resources that are important to humans. We have seen that everything in nature is a resource so we should extend our concern to all resources because each is valuable in its own right, playing a part in the workings of the world.

Diminishing resources

When we choose to use renewable resources we do not make an overall deduction from the Earth's wealth. But when we use non-renewable resources we are taking away something that cannot be replaced within a period that we could possibly imagine. On a human timescale fossil fuels, metals, rocks and even forests are not renewable. And yet we use these resources as though there were a limitless supply for our use, and with little regard for the pollution that we cause in the process.

Fossil fuels

Oil and coal play a large role in powering our lifestyles. But the thoughtless and inefficient use of these resources will threaten the inheritance of future generations in two ways. Firstly, the polluting effects of burning fossil fuels, which contribute to poor air quality, acid rain and the greenhouse effect, will jeopardise the health of the planet as a whole for decades to come. Secondly, the reserves may get used up, requiring us to draw on other sources of power.

When it comes to power, we need to match the right power source to the right job, making far greater use of clean power from the sun, wind and water. This will preserve fossil fuels for the jobs they are most appropriate for and reduce pollution.

Metals

Although metals cannot be destroyed, we waste them and damage the environment by spreading them throughout the world in quantities that poison ecosystems but are too thinly distributed to be recoverable. Some of the more popular metals in human use – like steel and aluminium – are recycled, but usually only when they are not mixed with any other materials. When metals form small parts of a complicated piece of electronic equipment they usually fall out of circulation. So an aluminium drinks container has every chance of being recycled but the equally valuable metals used in a watch, for example, will probably end up in a landfill.

Forests

I have already described the wealth of our forests. We can't treat them simply as sources of wood and wood pulp. Their wealth can't be defined in terms of the wood that they provide. All forests provide habitat, help preserve biodiversity, act as carbon sinks and play a role in the carbon cycle. Much of the value of a forest actually comes with age. And long established forests can't be recreated quickly!

Replacing old growth forests with single species plantations is not replacing like with like. Although paper and wood-pulp manufacturers are anxious to assure us that farming trees is a sustainable practice, the value of the forest is diminished. In fact it is no longer a forest but a monoculture that neither preserves biodiversity nor provides habitat for different species, nor does it act as a carbon sink because of the short life of the trees.

Rainforests belong to the country whose boundary they fall within, but the importance of these forests transcends national boundaries. Despite the fact that there may be a moral duty for the governments of rainforest nations to protect the forests for the benefit of the wider world, this often conflicts with the need or desire for economic growth within those countries. The trees may be the valuable resource that is plundered, or it may be just the land that is valued because once cleared it can be used to grow cash crops which are exported. In recent years the rainforests of Brazil and South East Asia have made international news as raging fires have taken their toll on the forest and its inhabitants (including the Yanomami – indigenous people who live in the rainforest in Brazil). The fires of South East Asia have had far reaching effects as huge quantities of smoke remained close to the ground and travelled as far as Western Australia (see box). However, the UK hardly has the moral right to protest, as we have already destroyed our own forests.

> ## The profit in loss
> In 1997–8 the rainforests of Indonesia were ablaze. In the main, fires are not accidental but a deliberate land clearing practice. For centuries slash-and-burn farming has been practised by smallholders without causing problems. But there is a difference in scale between clearing land for a smallholding and clearing land for a huge plantation. In 1997, as fires swept out of control (partly due to the weather), the Indonesian government appealed for the deliberate burning to stop. But the same government had policies which encouraged a huge expansion in plantation farming which involves clearing the forest. In addition, the price of timber has been kept low to the extent that it is cheaper to burn the trees than to harvest them for sale. The trees are not even valued as commodities and the forest is in a no-win situation.
>
> The profits go to plantation owners and the government. But the loss impacts on us all. In addition to the destruction of the fire, the smoke in 1997 affected an area 100 times greater than that actually burned. The health of an estimated 40,000 people was affected by the smoke, and plane crashes caused by the smoke cost almost 300 lives. The tourist industry will also have suffered economically.
>
> There are effects which go beyond even this. The unusually large quantity of smoke is accounted for by the fact that in many instances it wasn't just forest that was burning but the peat bogs on which some forests stand. Huge amounts of carbon are stored in the peat, which has been laid down over a period of 10,000 years and in places is over 20 m deep. This will considerably increase the levels of carbon dioxide in the atmosphere and only time will tell just how this will affect our climate.

Pollution

The desire and need for convenience and for efficient communications and mobility in our ever more hurried lives has brought us where we are today. Many of the things that we produce with the intention of benefiting humankind actually play a part in degrading the quality of the air, water and land. So, in addition to using up resources, we are also creating pollution. In other words, we are throwing away quality as well as quantity.

Chemical disaster

Large scale production of synthesised chemicals has been happening for over 60 years now, with scientists making new and previously unimaginable substances. There are currently 70,000 chemicals in commercial use and some of these are known to be carcinogenic (causing cancer), and/or mutagenic (causing genetic mutation). New chemicals undergo toxicological tests to determine their safety. There are many toxic chemicals in day-to-day use but they are considered safe for us to use because scientists have decided that there are 'tolerable daily intakes' (TDIs) that we can be subjected to.

In recent years public awareness has been raised about hormone disrupting chemicals or 'gender benders'. Hormones regulate body processes and help to maintain our health. They play an important role in reproduction and growth. We are both deliberately and accidentally producing hormone disrupting chemicals which are persistent in the environment and can easily find their way into our bodies (primarily through the food chain in the same way as DDT and dioxins). They mimic the chemistry of true hormones and fool the body into accepting them. Those that are created deliberately are often unnecessary and should be abandoned or replaced with a safe alternative. Those that are created by accident indicate a problem with another chemical in use which must be addressed.

Since 1991 studies have shown that at least 50 synthetic industrial chemicals can interfere with hormones and disrupt normal growth and development in birds, fish, reptiles, amphibians and mammals, including humans. We are still learning more about the threat that hormone disrupters pose. Possible effects to humans and other creatures include: changes in sexual preference and behaviour, reduced sperm count, cancers, nervous-system disorders, birth defects and damage to the immune system. This knowledge has been gained by assessing chemicals in isolation. However, they don't exist in isolation. It is estimated that there are between 300 and 500 artificial chemicals present in our bodies today. When some chemicals mix together there are synergistic effects – ie they have a much greater effect when they get together than that of the total of each chemical acting separately.

We should hear the alarm bells ringing. It's like history repeating itself. These chemicals mount up in soil, water and living creatures and they interfere with our capacity to reproduce. They reduce our potential to create healthy offspring.

Averting disaster

By taking responsible action to stop the deliberate production of dangerous chemicals we will be helping to ensure a healthy future for life on Earth. The Women's

Environmental Network, the World Wide Fund for Nature (WWF), Friends of the Earth and Greenpeace are all working on the issue of hazardous chemicals – contact them or visit their websites for more information.

Cars, roads and countryside

Perhaps the most publicised environmental issue of the past decade in Britain has been the building of new roads (and runways). The threat to ancient woodlands and sites of natural beauty has mobilised many people to protest. Eco-warriors are all ages and from all walks of life. They are united by the common aim to halt the spread of tarmac and petrol fumes across Britain.

Campaigners have been fighting to save green spaces (and their inhabitants) and protect human quality of life too. The natural environment is important for our emotional and spiritual well-being – to see things alive and growing is truly inspiring. Trees of great age with brand new shoots, flowers, foliage and gnarled roots; animals and insects that inhabit the natural space; all help to place us in the world. We can clear our heads and reorganise our perspective. There is something very humbling about wandering among ancient giants who were already old when our grandparents were babies.

We can touch flowers, hear the rustle of leaves and the snap of twigs underfoot; stroke velvety moss and trace our fingers over the patterns in tree bark. We can breathe in fresh air and smell the earth and rain – the scent of a flower might instantly send us back in time. The feel of the sun, wind and rain on our skin can remind us that there are things far more powerful than us mere mortals.

Walking in the countryside isn't like walking in the town. It isn't just about getting some exercise, but about experiencing the natural environment and exposing ourselves to the elements, free from the oppression of tall buildings and artificial noise. It's something that we experience emotionally and spiritually as well as physically.

As more and more land is covered by tarmac, concrete and motorway service stations, our lives are less rich, and less healthy too. But the encroachment of roads is a gradual process and the results are not obvious until it is too late. When trees are destroyed they no longer work to filter our polluted air while the ever increasing number of cars carried by our roads contribute to airborne pollution from petrol and diesel fumes. Respiratory conditions like asthma and bronchitis are aggravated by poor air quality caused by heavy traffic flow. And roads also damage our health much more directly, through road-traffic accidents.

Why do We Make so Much Waste?

Overconsumption

Humans aren't born wasteful, it's something that we learn. When we arrive in the world all we require is our mother's arms and breast. What we truly need – namely love and our mother's milk – cannot be bought. Yet as we grow we quickly assume the role of consumer, firstly through our parents and then in our own right. Most of us are guided into the habit of overconsumption before we are even aware of it. We are subject to many influences all around us, such as popular culture and advertising. In addition, our parents, peers, environment and our own personal search for knowledge and understanding all contribute to shaping our sense of the world. Our unique experiences lead us to form unique opinions, but it would be difficult for anyone to argue that making waste makes sense. Yet we make so much waste because we are conditioned to accept it as a by-product of modern life.

We've established that of all species on this planet we humans are the untidiest. We make things that don't biodegrade and we make too much. Western nations have followed a model of development that is concerned primarily with economics and money and takes little or no account of how things work in nature or of the interconnection of different living things. Our wasteful behaviour impacts negatively on the environment and negatively on humans as a part of that environment.

Industrial economies like ours in Britain revolve around the manufacture and sale of 'goods'. We are constantly being told, even from the language that we use, that buying things is right. Business thrives on repeated purchases, so building things with a long useful life is often seen as undesirable. Many items that we buy are designed with a limited lifespan in mind – this is known as 'built-in obsolescence'. One example that springs to mind is the toaster which can be built to last and to be easily repaired, but very few of them are. Think about how many toasters you have lived with! And where are they now?

Built-in obsolescence encourages us to view things as disposable – after all, what are you supposed to do with a toaster or a hairdryer or a kettle when it's kaput? But this is just the tip of the disposable iceberg. Contemporary

Britain is a throwaway society following fast on the heels of the USA. We can now choose to buy from a huge range of products designed to be used only once – sanitary towels, razors, cups, tissues, nappies, knickers, lighters and cameras are just a few of them.

Disposable products have been marketed in the name of convenience and cleanliness, and it has worked. We have come to accept, even to expect, disposability. The machinery of marketing has educated us not to care, not to think about the past or future of products and not to take responsibility.

The forces which drive consumerism are very strong. Developments in transport and communication mean that few destinations can escape the influence of corporate advertising. The purpose of adverts is to promote dissatisfaction. In less developed or non-industrial nations western lifestyle advertisments can sow the seeds of dissatisfaction in the psyche of an entire nation. Constant representations of different products and lifestyles can undermine traditional lifestyles and values.

Many multinational companies are richer and more powerful than most governments. They operate on a truly global level, picking and choosing which countries will provide the cheapest labour force to manufacture their products. Sometimes different production processes take place in different countries so products are transported around the world, even before they are ready for sale. When they are distributed they are sold right across the world to markets created by the advertising industry.

Education can help to inform people about the environmental impact of different products and lifestyles. Sometimes we need a little nudge to help us see what's right in front of us. We can be blinded by the social acceptability of wasteful products. In fact if you don't use some of them people can think you're a bit odd! However, armed with knowledge and a new awareness, consumers can help to halt and then reverse the wasteful, throwaway trend we have grown used to.

Sustainable development

This planet is our life support system and we have to live within its limitations. Limiting our activities because of the environment isn't something that comes naturally to us. We are clever creatures used to overcoming problems, and we are not used to accepting limits to our endeavours. In many ways this is a positive trait and has led to some incredible human achievements. On the other hand, if we get carried away with our own self-importance and disregard the delicate balance of our ecosystem we'll be heading for trouble.

If we are to safeguard the planet and our future on it then the way that each nation organises its society and develops its economy must be sustainable. Our lifestyles need to be durable and our vision should be long term. Sustainable development is about meeting the needs of present generations without threatening the ability of future generations to meet their needs.

Environmentalists have been talking about sustainable development for over 20 years, but since the Earth Summit in Rio in 1992 the term has come into popular usage. Organised by the United Nations, the Earth Summit was a forum for governments and non-governmental organisations (for example, pressure groups like the Women's Environmental Network) to debate and decide upon a plan of action for the twenty-first century. This plan is called Agenda 21. It is an enormous document that acknowledges the connection and interdependence of environmental, social and economic problems. In Britain every local authority has a Local Agenda 21 which details ways in which sustainable development can be put into practice locally, making social and economic progress but not at the expense of the environment.

Sustainable development requires us to consider the true value of the resources we make use of. To the indigenous peoples of the Americas and Australia the Earth is respected and is the focus of their spirituality. Activities like mining are considered a violation – like the rape of the Earth. The way that Native Americans made use of buffalo is a lesson in resourcefulness to us all. Killing only took place out of necessity and each kill provided food, materials for trading, clothing and shelter, thread for sewing, and tools fashioned from bones. Every part of the buffalo had its use. Outrageously, during the eighteenth century white men almost eliminated both the Native American and buffalo populations, committing mass slaughter and destroying an ecological balance that had been struck between humanity and another species.

If we don't use materials efficiently then we are creating waste on three levels:

- the energy used to extract them
- the actual resource
- the energy used to dispose of them.

Take as an example the use of disposable cups in canteens. The plastic is made from oil, so our oil reserves are reduced before we even think about the impact of extraction and transportation to a factory. Emissions to air from manufacture contribute to acid rain while those to water pollute our supply. Once made, more fossil fuels are used and air pollution caused as the cups are distributed for use. When the cups have been used once they are discarded into the rubbish bin and collected for disposal. The collection vehicle runs on fossil fuel and its emissions contribute to both the greenhouse effect and acid rain. It is most likely that the cups will end up in a landfill site where they will not rot but simply linger. The landfill will produce greenhouse gases, degrade the land and possibly contaminate groundwater with toxic leachate (an escaping cocktail of liquid nasties).

A more sustainable scenario would be to use durable cups or mugs which could be washed using the canteen's facilities and used over again. This would reduce demand on raw materials and prevent waste occurring at the end of every drink. Washing would have an environmental impact because it would require hot water and detergent, but the impact from these are local and more controllable. The 'proximity principle' (see page 16) is an important aspect of sustainability. It stresses the importance of waste being dealt with locally in order to minimise environmental impact.

Sustainable development requires the fair distribution of resources across the world as well as the conservation of resources for future generations. At present just 20 per cent of mainly western people consume over 80 per cent of the world's resources. These rates of consumption have already caused and continue to cause environmental damage, and yet it would be neither fair nor just to deny the other 80 per cent of the world's population the opportunity to reach the same material standard of living that most of us in the West enjoy. The sustainable path that we need to navigate is one that maintains the high standard of living of richer countries while making a drastic cut in the resources consumed by those countries. This will allow less developed countries fair access to resources to improve standards of living throughout their population as well as giving an inspiring example of sustainable resource management.

Personal development

You can contact your local council's Agenda 21 officer to find out how you and your school can get involved with putting sustainable development into practice.

Measuring a fair share – ecological footprinting

When scientists try to measure overall environmental impact it's often difficult to compare like with like. Disposable nappies use a lot of wood pulp and plastic made from oil. Washable nappies use few materials because they are reused, but need hot water and detergent to wash them. How can we make a proper comparison?

One approach that environmentalists have developed to overcome this problem is called 'ecological footprinting'. This imagines us having no fossil fuels but having to produce all our energy from sustainable sources. In each country we'd imagine that trees or other crops would be especially grown and burnt to produce energy to make products or alternatively, that trees are planted to absorb the CO_2 produced by fossil fuel – roughly the same area of land is needed in each case.

It's possible to work out the area of land needed for both energy production and material use for particular products. In the case of nappies, it was found that a larger area of land was needed for disposable nappies than washable ones. But (don't panic!) you don't have to wash the nappies yourself – laundries were found to be most resource efficient and used the smallest area of land.

When footprinting is done like this for whole countries, and includes food, material and energy use, industrial countries like Britain are using far more than their fair share of world resources. We do this by using up forests and mining land in other countries, and by burning fossil fuels which would require huge plantations to counteract their effect on global warming. In ecological footprinting terms we really have got far too big for our boots.

What are We Going To Do?

In the next chapters I'm going to look at ways that we can reduce the amount of waste we produce and at the same time improve our quality of life and the life of the planet as a whole. There is much that we can do as individuals, but we don't have to take the weight of the world on our shoulders – there are limits to our responsibilities and we have to call on governments and industry to be responsible too.

Much of the waste that we currently make could be avoided. Simple caretaking measures combined with innovative and creative thought and action can drastically reduce the waste that we currently make.

Chapter 2

Consuming and Using

We need to use resources to provide the basic necessities of food, shelter and clothing at the very least. There's nothing wrong with consumption in itself. We need to consume in order to function. But in Britain (and industrialised nations generally) we have neglected to consider the functioning of the planet – our support system – in our process of development. This oversight has allowed us to develop wasteful habits. We produce and consume far too many things without considering the full extent of their impact on the environment. We don't have to stop consuming and using, we just have to do it differently.

Avoiding waste isn't about having less of anything (except rubbish!). It's about getting more – more value, greater efficiency and a better quality of life. This chapter considers the role we can have as consumers and users in creating a less wasteful society, through positive use of purchasing power and user habits.

The Market Place

In Britain it is generally the so-called 'natural' market forces of advertising and supply and demand that determines what we will find in our shops. The theory is that if we all wanted to buy environmentally sound goods, then the shops would be full of them. There are some legal restrictions on certain hazardous products being made and sold, but there is a general reluctance by governments to regulate the market place. So to what extent can we as consumers vote with our purses and demonstrate our demand for no/low waste products?

You only have to take a look around a supermarket to see the incredible range of choice at our fingertips. But what choice are we really being offered? When you hassle your mum or dad to buy environmentally friendly washing powder and they say 'OK, which one is greenest?' What then? Have you ever studied the washing-powder aisle looking for the most environmentally friendly product? Lots of brands are made by the same companies and have virtually the same ingredients and most of them have huge amounts of phosphates (bad news for the environment). Availability of green products in supermarkets varies a lot and you might have to go to a health food shop or mail-order catalogue to get what you need. So, although we do have the opportunity to buy decent products, at the moment it takes more time and effort than just picking up a different carton at the supermarket.

The power of the purse is mighty and retailers and

manufacturers will respond to your demands as a customer, because their livelihood depends on it (see box for one example of this). So do make your demands known. To make effective purchasing decisions we need sufficient information in order to choose low waste products. We also need enough money and freedom from poverty in order to make ethical purchases, which are sometimes more expensive than more harmful alternatives.

> ### Purchasing power
> In the 1980s the public was told that CFCs (chlorofluorocarbons) in aerosol cans were a major contribution to thinning of the ozone layer in the atmosphere around the Earth to such an extent that there was actually a hole in the ozone over Antarctica. The job of this layer is to screen out some of the harmful ultraviolet rays emitted from the sun. We were warned that harmful rays would cause sunburn after very little exposure to the sun and it was predicted that an upsurge in skin cancer would take place. Today in Australia, which is in close proximity to the ozone hole, skin cancer is the next most common cancer after lung, breast and prostate cancer.
>
> On the basis of this information many people rejected aerosols and it didn't take long before manufacturers stopped producing aerosols propelled by CFCs. It's not really a fairy-tale ending though because, although the CFCs have gone, we still have aerosols with alternative propellants which pose a major waste problem because the cans can't be reused. Aerosols are one example of bad ecological design because they have a short working life and the resources from which they are made can't easily be recycled at the end of it, in addition to

> which there is nothing that is sold in an aerosol that couldn't be packaged differently. If as much publicity were given to the problems that aerosols cause in disposal as to the ozone layer, then perhaps we could eliminate them from the shelves completely.

Since the environmental movement emerged in the 1960s debates have raged about which products and processes cause more or less environmental damage. During the late 1980s and early 1990s, opinion polls recorded an upsurge in public interest in environmental matters, and this was reflected in the products people bought. 'Green' or 'environmentally friendly' products were hugely popular. Manufacturers and advertisers exploited public concern and supermarket shelves were awash with products that boasted green credentials.

Claims of greenness accompanied anything from light bulbs to loo roll. Some companies made legitimate claims but others were just hitching a ride on the green bandwagon. Green was a buzzword and for a while it could sell anything! Items which had never been hazardous were suddenly marketed as green just to boost sales and others were sold as environmentally friendly when the grounds for making such claims were shaky. Many people began to feel duped by green marketing and the bubble eventually burst. While for some it had educated and informed, for others it had simply confused.

Through the 1990s some efforts were made to clarify environmental claims. The public had demonstrated a willingness to respect the environment, but they weren't about to be led up the garden path by slick marketing. They wanted the truth. A scientific system of measuring environmental impact called 'life cycle analysis' (LCA) was developed to assesses the impact of a product from production to disposal. Comprehensive information like this allows comparisons between different products and processes and helps us determine which are least, or most, damaging. However, LCA doesn't always provide final answers, merely information which is subject to interpretation. Unlike ecological footprinting, LCA measures different impacts – eg the use of fossil fuels, water, raw materials – separately, so it can be difficult to achieve conclusive results when comparing different products or processes. The so-called 'nappy war' of the early 1990s was proof of that!

Battle of the nappies!

In the late 1980s, under increasing pressure from a rise in green consciousness, Procter & Gamble, the makers of Pampers nappies, commissioned two reports to give a life cycle analysis of disposable and reusable nappies. P&G wanted to counter the complaint from environmentalists that disposable nappies were far from disposable and more of a long term nuisance. On the basis of these reports P&G published a series of leaflets which claimed that there was little difference between the environmental impact of each type of nappy. They concentrated less on the issue of disposal and stressed the environmental impact of washing nappies.

In 1991 the Women's Environmental Network challenged these claims by making a formal complaint to the Advertising Standards Authority. This was backed up with evidence supplied by the Landbank Consultancy. WEN had commissioned the Landbank Consultancy (who were involved in developing life cycle analysis techniques) to produce a scientific critique of the studies funded by P&G. The report that they produced highlighted major errors in the interpretation and assumptions made to quantify the difference between disposable and reusable nappies. The Landbank Consultancy used the same raw data but arrived at very different conclusions. They found that disposables use 3–5 times as much energy, use up to 8.3 times more non-renewable raw materials and create 60 times as much domestic solid waste as washable nappies.

As a result, WEN's complaint was upheld and P&G had to withdraw their environmental claims. Since then WEN's campaign to promote real nappies and nappy washing services has developed considerably. The National Association of Nappy Washing Services now exists to co-ordinate the many nappy washing services that have been established, and the Real Nappy Association exists to promote the use of washable nappies in general.

In 1993, P&G commissioned a third life cycle analysis which concluded that regarding fossil-energy use, no significant difference between cloth and disposable nappies could be established. BUT this was without taking into account the energy derived from wood used to power the pulping process for disposables! This was discounted on the grounds that it was a renewable raw material!

In an attempt to counter confusing environmental information provided by manufacturers, a system of eco-labelling has been developed within the European

Union. This provides consumers with clear and accurate information about products they are considering to buy. This has been a very slow process, dominated by the manufacturers because they have the most resources, and sometimes delayed by disagreements and obstruction by companies. However, a growing number of products are being assessed for eco-labelling. In 1998, 180 products in nine EU countries carried the eco-label symbol, compared to just 40 in 1997.

Some European countries have established their own national eco-labelling schemes, for example Germany's 'Grune Punkt' (green dot) and The Netherlands' 'Milieukeur'. Britain doesn't have a national scheme at present, preferring to support the Europe-wide initiative.

In the 1980's the enormous demand for environmentally friendly products was branded green consumerism. Many people wanted to be seen to be green and wanted to buy all the products that would demonstrate their concern for the environment – a classic case of conspicuous consumption, one of the diseases of modern society that has caused environmental problems in the first place. Green consumerism is a paradox because the two ideas contradict each other. Using our purchasing power discerningly and choosing things which have minimal impact on the environment can be a very powerful tool but having an environmental conscience is as much about the things that we reject as the things that we select. Green consumption means buying recycled tissues whereas being green means using a cotton handkerchief.

As a population our environmental concern seems to be gradually increasing in a solid way which will not be shaken. This is due in part to the commitment of young people to make the environment a priority. The 1997 National Consumer Council Survey divided the population into five groups on the basis of their environmental actions. The groups were:

- affluent greens   19 per cent
- recyclers   19 per cent
- careful spenders   19 per cent
- young greens   17 per cent
- sceptics   26 per cent.

The young greens are a mixture of students and unemployed people on very low incomes. Despite not having very much money young greens have a strong commitment to buying environmentally friendly products even though they think they are more expensive than 'normal' products.

Disposable Products

We call one-use items 'disposable' and don't think twice about throwing them away. Using valuable resources to make and sell things which are used once and then discarded doesn't make ecological sense. Resources are used up and a mountain of rubbish is created – how disposable is that? It doesn't disappear – it has to be dealt with. The only thing we are really disposing of is our responsibility.

So, why do we have throwaways if they are such a bad idea? Well, there is always more than one way of looking at things and everybody has their own idea of what makes sense. Opinions differ between ecologists and economists — things that make ecological sense don't always make economic sense. When there is a conflict of interests and the environmental option appears to be most expensive this is usually because we are taking a very short term view and not adequately valuing the environment that supports us.

We have been sold on the idea that disposable products are easy and that we need them in order to keep pace with our busy lifestyles. They offer us convenience. They don't need looking after or taking care of. They make virtually no demands on our time and energy. They can also operate as status symbols because disposable products offer us an escape from tasks and activities which are considered menial, like washing. In the case of sanitary towels and nappies it's also a way of minimising involvement with bodily fluids and waste — things which in our culture we are not very good at dealing with.

Deciding Where to Spend your Money

You may want to use your purchasing power to select the shops you use as well as the individual items. To assess a company's environmental credentials you will need to do a little investigating. Depending on the size of the shop, you may do this in person or by writing or telephoning for information. Consider the response you get. Does the response actually tell you what you want to know? Have your questions been answered and is your curiosity really satisfied?

Many companies in operation today do have an environmental policy. If asked by a member of the public most companies will explain that of course they are concerned about the environment (who wouldn't be?) and they are doing all they can to operate in a sustainable way. Much of this is gloss – a public relations exercise to keep consumers happy – which has little meaning in real terms. Companies are in business primarily to make money. Some are genuinely enlightened and have additional concerns such as social justice and the environment. Most have money making as their sole goal.

Don't be afraid to dig a little deeper than the public relations department might want you to. It's easy to send out glossy public information leaflets – they advertise the company and don't usually contain much information. Answering letters containing specific questions takes time and effort. A company that really values their customers will answer their questions. A company that really values the environment will stand up to your scrutiny because they will have already thought about and acted upon the issues. It's becoming more common for companies to promote themselves as socially and environmentally conscious – look out for those that do.

These are some of the questions you can ask:

- Do they have a waste-reduction policy and if so, what is it?
- Do they use any reusable packaging?
- Do they recycle their pre-consumer packaging?
- Do they have on-site recycling facilities for staff and customers to use – eg to recycle post-consumer packaging from their goods?
- Do they use recycled stationery?
- Do they use proper crockery and cutlery in the staff

room/canteen or disposables?
- Do they compost any canteen waste?
- Do they have any refill schemes?
- Do they sell local produce with minimum packaging?
- Do they freely give out carrier bags or do they encourage customers to bring their own?

You can tailor your letter to suit the recipient. Explain that you are concerned about the environment and keen to support companies that take a responsible attitude and minimise their output of waste. One letter may generate a fairly standard response – which might not actually answer your questions – press the company until you are satisfied that your queries have been answered.

Big Versus Small – Keep it Local!

Over the last century the way that we shop in Britain has been changing, but the past 20 years in particular have witnessed rapid and drastic changes to the way we shop. Pedestrians have become less well served as village and high-street shops are overshadowed by out-of-town retail parks. Town and country planning of shopping facilities has increased dependence on cars despite our awareness of pollution problems and road-traffic accidents.

It isn't just the physical location of shops that has changed. Their size, character and role in the community has too. Self-serve superstores can provide low priced goods because buying in bulk gives a cheaper unit price and huge purchasing power enables them to get lower prices out of suppliers. Big stores buy huge amounts of goods and can afford to sell them at very competitive prices. Supermarkets have marketed themselves as closer to the warehouse; big DIY stores in particular.

Throughout Britain we are increasingly served by chain stores that offer a standardised experience. We may find security in the familiar but we're missing out on the regional diversity that independent shops offer. We are losing variety and our culture is less rich as a result. Large shops can be very impersonal and even stressful for shoppers. For workers, jobs can be very boring.

On offer in our shops in Britain we have an unprecedented variety of things to buy. As far as food is concerned we import from every continent allowing an international flavour to any table. The speed at which fresh produce can be transported has virtually rendered seasonal produce a thing of the past. Shelves are so well stocked all the year round that we are less and less aware of what foods are in season in Britain at any one time. As we become less dependent on local growing patterns it is more difficult for us to appreciate that we are simply part of nature. We get short sighted and begin to think of *shops* as being the source of our food instead of the Earth. Acknowledging where our food comes from reminds us of the natural scheme of things and can spark an unexpected response of excitement and connection with the rest of the world that is unfamiliar in most of our daily lives.

Importing food from across the world creates tonnes of air pollution and requires food to be chemically treated to keep it looking attractive. The chain of food transportation begins at the farm and includes travel on lorries, ships, planes, lorries again and then usually home in a car. Supermarkets have one or two distribution centres for the whole country. Locally grown produce may go a hundred miles to the centre and then back again. The distance between where a food is grown and where it is eaten is calculated in 'food miles'. Keeping food miles to a minimum reduces pollution that contributes to global warming, ozone depletion, child cancers and heart and lung disease. It also reduces demand on the natural resources required for transportation and packaging.

There are other prices to be paid for importing both exotic and familiar foods. We import a lot of food from the Third World where cheap labour and land are exploited by large companies which grow cash crops in monoculture plantations for export to the West. The production of food for export is given priority over growing food for local consumption because it is profitable for large land owners. This can lead to local food shortages and the obscene situations that occur when countries struck by famine continue to export food to the West. For example, during the Ethiopian famine 1984–5 food crops were still being exported to the West while harrowing pictures of starving people were shown on our televisions and Bob Geldof was organising Band Aid to raise money to ease the food 'shortage'.

Many of our staple foods are cash crops grown in monoculture conditions. Tea, coffee, sugar and cocoa are classic examples. Unless we buy these products organically grown and fairly traded we are supporting unsustainable agriculture which uses vast amounts of pesticides. This puts farm workers at risk from pesticide poisoning and compromises the health of the consumer. It is worth bearing in mind that some of those really nasty chemicals like DDT are still widely used in countries such as India and China.

Traditionally our shops were independent or part of a very small chain. This is now increasingly rare. Specialist shops serving the local community – for example, bakers, greengrocers, hardware stores and timber merchants – can offer specialist knowledge, advice and a personal service in addition to the products for sale. Independent stores can be more flexible than chain stores – they will often order in specific items at your request and can respond much more quickly to suggestions to collect recyclables or compostables, or to set up refill schemes for some products. Basically they can make their own decisions and don't have to wait for head office to tell them what they can or can't do.

Small shops might be a little more expensive than the warehouse-type ones but we should consider what it is we are paying for. We tend to undervalue things which evade financial quantification such as personal service and atmosphere, yet it is often these apparently valueless things which can really make a difference.

Local shops have a great deal to offer us. They could be the focus of many waste saving initiatives. Having shops within easy walking distance would help to persuade shoppers to leave their cars at home, minimising fuel use and pollution. Stocking local produce would minimise the impact of transportation and require less packaging. Reuse of packaging, refill schemes, recycling and composting could all operate as positive examples of waste minimisation. In the village of Wye in Kent small shopkeepers play an important part in Wyecycle – a community waste minimisation business.

★

Wyecycle

The village of Wye in Kent is a fine example of how, with a little encouragement, we can massively reduce the waste we produce whilst helping to recreate sustainable communities. Thanks to the facilities that Wyecycle has established, residents can reduce their rubbish by 90 per cent of the national average (from 1000 kg to 100 kg).

Wyecycle co-ordinates recycling but its main objective is to reduce waste through promoting careful purchasing, reuse and composting. Recycling is definitely seen as a last resort and plastics recycling is rejected altogether on the grounds that we should be avoiding or reusing plastics because recycling has no benefits to offer (see recycling section, p87).

Glass, paper, cardboard, tins, cans, textiles and engine oil are collected for recycling on a weekly basis. Organic kitchen and garden waste are also collected weekly for composting. Furniture, paint, wood and other miscellaneous items are collected on a monthly basis. In the village shop a refill scheme for household cleaning products is in operation in conjunction with Wyecycle. Other plastic waste can be reduced by purchasing soft drinks in returnable glass bottles from the corner shop, and by avoiding plastic bags and over packaged goods where possible.

The most recent addition to Wyecycle's waste saving activities is the veggie-box scheme – a joint venture with a local organic farmer. The box scheme provides a stable, regular market for the farmer and healthy, sustainably produced, unpackaged food for subscribers to the scheme. Box schemes are a great way of reducing food miles and food packaging.

Organic box schemes are becoming more popular as a cheap and convenient way of buying organic food. Most schemes serve a fairly small area and weekly deliveries are made to a collection point from which participants can collect their food. Ideally the food is always supplied by a local organic farmer, thus keeping food miles to an absolute minimum. The commitment of participants provides valuable security for the organic farmer who has a far more precarious existence than mainstream farmers who receive government subsidies. Some schemes are supplemented with imported food to maintain a variety of produce right through the year. A few operate as a nationwide delivery service which can be called upon at any time. These require no commitment, involve more transportation and are more costly, although they still keep packaging to a minimum (contact the Soil Association for details of your nearest scheme).

Farmers' markets also work to bring growers and consumers closer together, providing local food to local people. Farmers bring their produce direct to market so consumers don't have to pay for the profits of wholesalers and retailers. The food is fresh, food miles are low and packaging is minimal. Farmers and shoppers alike get a good price at minimal cost to the environment. In a few short years farmers' markets have become very popular and they are springing up all across Britain. Look out for an event near you. You might be surprised at the diversity of things you'll find, from honey and herbs to cheese and wine and lots more in between.

'Pick your own' schemes are another alternative to shops, which can be less wasteful and more fun. Many farms are introducing them. You simply pay for as much as you pick. This brings consumers in direct contact with food, as it grows, and minimises the packaging required.

It enables people who don't or can't grow food to keep in touch with agricultural seasons and life in the countryside. Farmers benefit by saving money on harvesting, packaging and transportation.

Old Versus New

Supporting our established second-hand businesses is an excellent way of minimising waste, maximising resource efficiency, and often saving money too. From junk shops, flea markets and charity shops to specialist second-hand traders, antique shops and auctions, we have in place many businesses that deal in used goods.

We can help supply the second-hand market by selling or donating our unwanted things instead of putting them in the bin. And we can create demand by making some of our purchases second-hand ones. You don't always have to use a middleman for your sales. You can sell directly to others through the small ads in the local paper, at a boot fair or by having a tabletop sale at home with your friends.

The charity sector

Charity shops represent a major reuse and recycling network in the UK. They mostly deal in used clothing, but most also have a selection of books, games and household items. You can find all sorts of weird and wonderful things!

> **Oxfam**
> Oxfam is probably the first name that springs to mind. Originating in 1947 as the Oxford Committee for Famine Relief with one shop to its name, Oxfam has now

> changed out of all recognition. In the UK and Ireland, 850 shops staffed mostly by volunteers sell donated clothes and goods to raise money for projects in developing countries, supporting and enabling poor communities in their efforts to raise their standard of living. Oxfam also provides emergency relief in times of crisis.

Charity shops provide an effective system of waste avoidance, though supporting them has benefits which extend beyond this. It raises money and awareness for good causes, is helpful to bargain hunters and people on low incomes and helps to make second-hand shopping socially acceptable throughout society. To this end, Oxfam have a shop in Ganton Street, Central London called No Lo Go which sells only donated designer wear. This helps lift the sometimes dull, down-at-heel image of charity shops to new glitzy heights and reminds us that second hand doesn't equal poor quality or second best.

There is some concern that clothing which is exported for sale in developing countries (because there is no market for it here) distorts local economies because cheap second-hand imports undermine the market for locally made garments. The availability of Western-style clothing can also work to undermine indigenous culture and experience. Complicated histories mean that developing countries have been encouraged to see 'West as best'. We shouldn't be encouraging this view – it's important to allow every nation to take pride in its own past, present and future, and to develop independently. Exported clothes have a role in emergency relief efforts but we should be cautious not to undermine or suppress local manufacturing initiatives and indigenous cultures.

If you haven't yet experienced charity shopping, try it now. It's good fun and it doesn't break the bank.

> You can avoid binning your unwanted textiles by:
> - taking them to a charity shop
> - depositing them in a clothing bank
> - contributing to door-to-door collections for charity
> - supplying a local jumble sale.

Oxfam shops also provide an outlet for Fairtrade goods. These are foods and crafts bought directly from producers in the Third World at a fair price which provides a decent living. This contrasts starkly with the working conditions and wages provided by many multinational companies that operate in developing countries specifically to exploit their cheap labour. Buying Fairtrade goods is shopping with a social conscience.

Mending and second-hand spending

Buying mended, refurbished or restored goods (such as furniture, electrical and electronic items) is another way of conserving financial and material resources. Many people already earn a living by mending and selling things but job opportunities could dramatically increase if we, the general public, decide to support such initiatives. Our responsibility as consumers needs to be matched by responsibility on the part of producers in order to make buying second hand an attractive proposition. Building things that last and can be mended will make the second-hand goods market more attractive because function and appearance will not diminish so rapidly.

One example which demonstrates the benefits of reusing rather than discarding old household appliances is CREATE – a community recycling project for 'white goods' in Liverpool. CREATE stands for Community Recycling Enterprise And Training for Employment. It's a scheme offering paid training to the long term unemployed through recycling and reuse of household appliances. Washing machines, fridges, dishwashers and the like are refurbished and are offered for resale in the local community. CREATE has plans to set up more schemes around Britain.

This scheme and others like it offer these benefits:
- **Waste reduction**
  Every year we throw away huge amounts of electrical appliances and gadgets. Many of these are either in working order or need fairly simple repairs. By salvaging items which would have been thrown into landfill we are extending their lives. By doing so we are reducing our demand for waste disposal and our demands for raw materials for new goods.
- **Job creation**
  The repair and resale of discarded items does more than create jobs. It allows people to develop skills which will give them greater access to the job market in the future. There are long term benefits for individuals and communities.
- **Cheaper goods**
  Refurbished goods offer a cheaper alternative to new

goods. They are sold to the general public, social services and welfare-rights organisations. Some are given away.

If you know someone who is about to replace old 'white goods' or furniture, you could encourage them to find out if they can donate their old goods to a local scheme, charity or the local council so that they can be reused rather than landfilled. Contact your local recycling officer at the council.

Computers

Famed for the speed at which they become obsolete, there are limits to upgrading them, and when these have been reached they slip further and further behind the times and soon become redundant. But not all of these machines are getting dumped. There is a very welcome industry initiative from the computer company ICL. They are taking back old computers and supplying them to approved recyclers who resell the majority to the second-hand market and strip down and recycle as much as possible from the remainder.

The feedback from recyclers is that designers and manufacturers need to be more aware of the computer afterlife and produce machines that are easy to dissemble with materials that can be recycled. When all manufacturers instigate take-back policies and adjust designs to make recycling easier and more efficient, the 'computer graveyard' will be a thing of the past.

Bytes Twice is the Association of Community Computer Reuse Projects. If your school or college is upgrading its computers, check with your headteacher or principal that the old ones aren't going in a skip. If they don't have a good home to go to contact Bytes Twice care of Waste Watch (see Resources).

Tools For Self-Reliance

This is a network of groups that refurbishes tools, packs them into kits, and sends them off for use in poorer nations. Tool kits have a number of destinations – for example, trade schools, boat-builders, women's groups, blacksmiths and refugees. Tools are vital to enable people suffering poverty, war and/or natural disaster to rebuild their lives. If friends, family or school are having a clear out don't let any useful equipment go to waste, contact the TFSR national office for details of your nearest group.

Book Aid

This organisation works along similar lines. Unwanted books or magazines that are needed in libraries of developing countries can be donated for redistribution. Your school or local library may be able to offer donations. You can contact Book Aid for more information.

Swapping and trading

Materials exchanges are another way of keeping resources in circulation. British industry produces huge amounts of waste every year. But waste from one company can be a raw material to another. To take full advantage of this situation and maximise economic and environmental advantage, systems of materials exchange have been developed by private companies such as WES (Waste Exchange Services) Recycling. A directory of available waste products is compiled and continually updated – products can be anything from egg shells to sulphuric acid. The directory creates a forum for businesses to both sell and buy surplus products. The emphasis is increasingly on – '*material*' rather than '*waste*'. This encourages us to value materials for their future potential rather than for past glories.

Such a system reduces disposal costs, is financially rewarding in itself, and allows the reuse of materials. More systems of this kind need to be developed in order for British business and industry to work at maximum efficiency by making waste work to the best possible advantage. In the age of the internet and the easy access to information and communication that it provides, we should be taking full advantage of the opportunity to operate economically and efficiently.

Scrap stores

The concept of materials exchanges can be applied to all sorts of situations, not just business and commerce. Scrap stores are an established idea. This is where suitable industrial scraps, such as paper, card, plastic and wood offcuts, paint and textiles, are passed on to a scrap club and then given or sold very cheaply to playgroups and schools for use as arts and crafts materials. If you could benefit from a scrap store or know someone who might be able to donate, contact the Community Recycling Network to find out if you have a local facility.

Boxing clever!

Calderdale and Kirklees Green Business Network has set up a waste exchange for local businesses which includes a scheme for redundant cardboard boxes. Some boxes are sold to a dealer for reuse. Some of the boxes that can't be reused are shredded and sold as animal bedding. The used animal bedding and associated manure are sold as compost. Boxes that aren't good enough quality for animal bedding are nonetheless shredded and form part of the diet of worms that are bred commercially for use in wormeries. By working together, the members of the network have managed to transform rubbish into a commercially valuable resource.

Student exchange

Community Recycling in Southwark Project (CRISP), in conjunction with South Bank University in London, has set up a pilot project to reduce waste in a college hall of residence. By the end of their stay many students have accumulated things which they no longer require or are unable to take with them for practical reasons (this especially applies to overseas students). The project aims to prevent unnecessary waste by redistributing items to other students or to a network of community recyclers if there are no takers among the students. The project is managed by the students themselves and if successful it will act as a model for every other college.

The London Woodbank

This organisation receives quality wood from theatres and businesses and sells it on cheaply to community organisations, artists and training schemes. A network of similar schemes could be established which could provide a vital resource for young artists and carpenters in need of cheap or free materials.

★

Home-grown ideas

Boot and garage sales are another example of waste exchange, as is selling in the small ads in the local paper. If you have old things you no longer need, you have a number of options which avoid putting them in the bin. Donating to the local charity shop is a good choice – your old things can be sold and the money used to help others in need. Alternatively you could try a garage, boot or tabletop sale to raise money for charity or your own funds. Another option, might be an internet exchange system. If you have things you want to get rid of, the chances are other people will have too. Perhaps it would be possible to set up an exchange page on a school or college website? This might be a fun way of integrating environmental studies with an information-technology project. With enthusiasm and energy the possibilities for waste exchange are countless.

Packaging

Rip it off!

The swell of consumerism through the 1980s made packaging an environmental issue for the 1990s. In 1991 the Women's Environmental Network launched its 'Wrapping is a Rip Off' Campaign to highlight the issue of over-packaging. This involved providing the public with information about the wastefulness of excess and inappropriate packaging, and asking them to use their power as consumers to persuade retailers and manufacturers to make less waste and take greater responsibility for the resources they use.

The campaign was punctuated by a number of organised actions at supermarkets and other food stores which were targeted for their huge contribution to packaging waste. The formula was simple yet effective. Individuals and groups took their shopping through the checkout and then removed the excess packaging, explaining what they were doing and leaving the wrappings for the store to dispose of. This tactic forced shops to consider their attitude towards packaging. Often people invited the local press to photograph the surplus packaging outside the store. It wasn't a silent boycott that might not get heard, but a practical demonstration which left unnecessary packaging in the hands of the retailer – the message was conveyed loud and clear.

Bring Your Own Bag – BYOB

There has been a general increase in awareness of packaging issues since that time. Lots of people take reusable bags or boxes for their shopping. Some shops ask you if you really need a bag (when a few years ago they couldn't give enough away) and Sainsbury's even gives you a penny back for every new bag that you *don't* use.

Some of the big supermarkets are offering a DIY shopping system where you scan your own goods as you go round the shop with a portable scanner and then just pay the total when you have finished. This truly must be twenty-first century shopping! Because you don't have to unload your shopping for an assistant to scan, you use the same reusable plastic cartons (which attach to special trollies) to pack your things in as you take them off the shelf and to take your shopping home. You might ask your parents to consider this as a way of saving the mountain of plastic carrier bags accumulating in kitchen drawers and cupboards!

Retailer responsibility required!

Even if we reject all packaging of goods from the shop, packaging is still required to protect goods travelling from manufacturer to retailer. The further goods travel and the more they are processed, the more packaging they generally require. Packaging protests of the early 1990s, and continued campaigns, have prompted some large stores to assess all types of packaging they use and some changes have been made to reduce packaging waste and increase efficiency. It's now not unusual to see goods waiting in reusable plastic crates to be stacked on shelves where not so long ago they would simply be in cardboard boxes.

Positive moves

Some people are making fundamental changes by simply choosing to avoid the supermarket altogether in an effort to reduce waste. Buying unpackaged bread from the baker, loose veg. from the greengrocer, draught beer at the pub etc. If you enquire at your local independent wholefood/healthfood shop you will probably find that you can buy food in bulk at a discount price while also minimising packaging. This can work well for college students who are short on funds but can find plenty of people to buy a share of the goods. Some shops, like the chain Weigh and Save, keep packaging to a minimum by buying in bulk and offering goods (such as cereals, pulses, nuts and seeds) for sale in large containers from which customers can scoop the desired quantity of each product.

Producer responsibility

Reducing packaging waste is not just the responsibility of consumers. We can avoid over-packaged items, shop selectively, recycle the recyclables but there will still be a residue of packaging that we have no use for and have to throw away. This is where producer responsibility comes in.

> **Legal requirements**
> As a result of European law, Parliament has introduced regulations regarding packaging waste. Basically this means that businesses involved in packaging have to take responsibility for the materials they use by recovering and recycling a percentage of them. Targets apply to six materials: aluminium, glass, paper (and board), plastic, steel and wood. These regulations help to promote greater environmental responsibility, and invariably they will save the businesses money! Even when capital investment is required for new equipment, the payback time is usually short and then the financial benefit of waste savings are felt. Waste saving changes often stemming from creative and lateral thought are simple and cost free.

Products also need to be designed with waste minimisation in mind. A brilliant example of a low-waste product is solid shampoo which needs only a paper wrapping at the point of sale. I first discovered shampoo bars at the Covent Garden branch of the cosmetics chain 'Lush' where wondrous great cakes of soap and shampoo are sold by weight just like at the delicatessen! The majority of products have little or no packaging, nothing is tested on animals, everything is vegetarian and vegan items are clearly marked. Hemp shampoo bars are also available by mail order from the Natural Collection catalogue (see Resources).

More recent additions to the Lush range are face packs not only *containing* fresh fruit and vegetables, but also *packaged* in them! Check these out for the ultimate in compostable packaging!

Another low waste product is the deodorant crystal. They are produced by a variety of companies and are available through wholefood shops and also in the Natural Collection catalogue. It is a lump of crystal (ammonium alum) that you apply to your armpits straight after washing before you are dry (or you can wet the crystal and apply). A fine deposit of crystal is left on your skin – it doesn't smell, it isn't sticky, your skin can still breathe, it is very effective and lasts for ages.

Refill Systems

Refill systems are an old idea that need to be revived. They don't just save waste, they serve to remind us that resources are precious, and help us to value the container as well as the contents.

Drink bottles

Up until the early 1970s all drink bottles were made from glass and 'deposits' were common. A refund of a few pence was available for each glass bottle that was returned to the shop where it was purchased. The bottle would then return to a local bottling plant where it would be washed and refilled (in the same way that milk bottles still are).

The organisation of materials in this way did more than just conserve resources. It encouraged us to value materials more highly and to think of them as something we have on loan, a bit like a library book which we borrow and then return. Deposit systems started fading away when bottling plants became more centralised, and lightweight, unbreakable plastic bottles became the favoured packaging for many drinks. We chuck these bottles away because we are encouraged not to value them but to think of them as disposable, and very few facilities exist to recycle them.

Refillable glass bottles need to be made from thicker glass than non-refillables so that they are tough enough to withstand industrial cleaning and sterilising. So refillables require more resources to start with, but repeated washing requires less energy and resources than recycling or making bottles from scratch.

Many people now buy supermarket own-brand goods rather than branded names from small shops. The old bottle-deposit schemes used to work through these small outlets sending full and empty bottles back and forth from manufacturer to retailer. New deposit schemes could operate in the same way, but they could also take off with considerable momentum through the national network of supermarkets that exists. That is if the supermarkets wanted to make that happen. It isn't something that is currently on their agendas. Perhaps not enough people have suggested that refill schemes and/or bottle deposits would be a good idea?

Changes can arise through decisions made from 'above' (the government) as well as 'below' (consumers). Governments can guide the behaviour of individuals and corporations by introducing legislation which sets out in detail rights and responsibilities in relation to waste. Overstepping rights or failing to fulfill responsibilities could result in a penalty. In Denmark disposable bottles were banned in 1979. Over 150 million bottles are returned every year and refilled on average 32 times. In Ontario, Canada, legislation has ensured that 30 per cent of all soft drinks must be sold in refillable bottles.

Milk round

How often are you asked to just nip out and get some milk? Having your milk delivered means that you don't have to! Milk rounds have been operating for decades but they have been on the decline in recent years. These are a valuable service which we need to support if we are not to lose them. Electric powered milk floats cause minimal pollution and they provide doorstep delivery of a small range of groceries, not just milk. Some also sell orange juice in 'milk' bottles. There is scope for developing this service to include other drinks and organic milk if there is sufficient demand. Take the initiative and find out for your parents what your local milk delivery service has on offer.

> Milk bottles are probably the best known example of a refill scheme. On average milk bottles are used 12 times, but this figure takes into account breakages and bottles that go missing (perhaps inadvertently recycled), so many bottles are used far more times than this.

Clean and green

Ecover is a company producing a variety of cleaning agents (washing-up liquid, washing powder etc) which are minimally damaging to the environment. They have a purpose-built eco-factory in Belgium. You can write to them for more information about their green business (see Resources). Ecover products are available from many wholefood and healthfood shops as well as some supermarkets. There is a refill system for some of their goods so you can use the same container over and over again, so long as you fill up with the same product. This service is not available in any supermarkets. Ask at your local healthfood shop if they offer this service or would consider setting up a system. If you can encourage people into the shop to use the system you might even get yourself (or your parents) a discount! The Magpie home delivery service in Brighton includes an Ecover refill system (see Resources if you're local).

Come again cosmetics
The Body Shop takes responsibility for its packaging and offers a refill service to its customers. Bottles are made from plastic and must be refilled with the original product and a 10 per cent discount is given for reusing the container. As well as a price cut, you get a card on which to collect refill stickers. Each bottle you refill gets you a sticker, and when you've collected six stickers you get a free product (from a selected range). Can't go wrong there! Containers that cannot be refilled are taken back and recycled into other items which are sold in the shop.

If you want to find out more about The Body Shop you can go on The Body Shop Tour in Littlehampton (West Sussex). It could provide useful material for a school project, or just offer a fun day out with friends (see Resources).

Neal's Yard Remedies is another company that takes a responsible approach to packaging. They sell cosmetics and herbs from a number of shops and also by mail order.

They supply most of their products in beautiful blue glass bottles and jars and they take back their packaging and recycle it into other products. You can refill bottles at the Covent Garden shop but there isn't a general refill policy. Purchases are wrapped in tissue and placed in brown paper bags. The goods are pricey but reflect the quality of the ingredients and small scale production.

In Britain refill schemes are few and far between and are often complicated by company bureaucracy (there are restrictions placed on what containers can be refilled and with what). A few years ago I came across a no-frills refill scheme in a small town in Australia where a shop was selling a variety of liquid goods such as shampoo, conditioner, washing-up liquid etc. The shop was lined with large vats of different coloured liquids from which you could fill your container. It appeared to be very flexible and customer friendly in comparison to schemes in operation here. Perhaps we need to follow this example for refill schemes to really take off in Britain.

Reuse Systems

Bring your own mug

Fast food and drinks offer convenience but they also encourage us to be thoughtless. Empty cups and cartons are soon discarded and add to our mountain of waste. But it doesn't have to be that way.

In the USA the idea of carrying your own cup to use for takeaway drinks is common among students and commuters who make regular visits to the same cafes. The cafe provides the cup and then a discount is given every time you use it and avoid using a disposable one.

You keep the cup and save money as well as waste.

But these schemes aren't an ocean away. The concept has already been introduced right here in Britain. There are two coffee-house chains in London that offer commuter cups and there are some independent examples. There is great potential for this kind of scheme to flourish in all sorts of settings. If you think your school or a favourite haunt could benefit from such a scheme why not suggest it? If your idea gets support you could organise a competition to design the reusable cup. Maybe the winner could get free refills?

There are advantages all round. The mugs serve as an advert for the shop or college and they can promote themselves as environmentally conscious. The shop is praised for offering reusables, and they don't even have to wash the cups up! The customer gets a discount, a cup, and the satisfaction of setting a positive example by not adding to the waste problem.

If people take the opportunity to use these initiatives, they will develop and grow. The fast-food industry could seize the opportunity to change its image of being resource wasteful and major litter contributors.

Mugs at festivals

Festivals and other one-off public events invariably involve a whole host of food and drink stalls offering refreshments in some shape or form. Cups, plates, napkins, knives, forks and spoons are all provided, and they are nearly always disposables.

The Tiny Tea Tent offers a lovely alternative. You'll find the Tea Tent at many festivals and gatherings in Britain and it provides more than a quick cuppa in a plastic beaker. Inside the tent, chairs and tables are a welcome resting spot. You are invited to enjoy a proper cup of tea from a lovely mug (from the mug tree). A wooden plaque explains why your tea will not be served in a throwaway cup. It's a nice space and it brings back a little of the ceremony traditionally associated with tea drinking.

The Tiny Tea Tent is the exception rather than the rule, and outdoor events create enormous amounts of rubbish. The 1999 Glastonbury Festival alone produced 1000 tonnes of waste for landfill (a further 40 tonnes were recycled).

Low waste festivals: Germany sets example

In Nuremberg, Germany in 1990 the local authority introduced a by-law aimed at reducing waste and maximising recycling. Part of the law made it illegal to use disposable cutlery and crockery at outdoor events. This affected the hot wine festival which runs for four weeks at Christmas time every year. It is a famous event and attracts around three million visitors. The previous year (1989), around 700,000 throwaway plastic cups were used to serve the hot wine.

The 1990 festival was rather different! The hot wine was served in washable ceramic cups and a central dishwashing area was arranged. The cups and dishwasher were paid for by the stallholders' profits. The customer paid a deposit on the cups which they could claim back.

It turned out that people weren't claiming their deposits back because they were keeping the cups as souvenirs! This worked out alright because the deposit was more than the cost of the cups to the stallholders. So profits were being made on the cups as well as the wine. The following year the design on the cup was

> changed to encourage people to add to their collection of souvenirs!
> This is just one of the measures that has led to Nuremberg making considerable reductions in the quantity of waste that it produces each year.

The Women's Environmental Network is working to promote low-waste indoor and outdoor events in a similar way. A Green Conference Pack is available which includes tips and information on how to put on an event with minimal waste. If you are involved in organising an event or meeting, or you know someone who is, think about what sort of waste might be produced and how you can minimise it. Contact WEN for more information.

WEN has also arranged for the management of Old Spitalfields Market in the East End of London to participate in the North East London Waste Minimisation and Management Project (NELWMMP). The project involves 15 businesses each working towards reducing the waste that they make.

The market is a public space visited by a wide variety of people. During the week the main customers are city workers crowding in for lunch from the many food stalls. On Sundays the market is busy with all sorts of people buying and browsing amongst the organic food stalls, second-hand clothes, books and bric-a-brac.

Markets produce a lot of waste. It's planned that the many food and drink stallholders who currently use a huge amount of disposable items (cups, plates, cutlery etc) will invest in reusable cutlery and crockery and purchase a dishwasher for communal use. This type of initiative coupled with some on-the-spot publicity of the project will work as a public-information and education exercise, which will in turn help to further minimise waste in other markets and beyond.

Round and round the garden

Thompson's plant and garden centres have invested in a colour-coded reuse system. The different coloured pots have nothing to do with reuse – they just cleverly indicate the type of plant and whereabouts in the garden it should be planted. Customers are asked to return the pots after planting out so that they can be used again.

Nappies

Nappies make up 4 per cent of domestic waste. So-called 'disposables' have made such an impact on parents and carers that to many people nappy washing is a laughing matter, a thing of the past. But design and technology have moved on. The reusable nappy has reinvented itself for the twenty-first century and offers a positive step into the future, not a walk back to the past.

Modern reusables are shaped like disposables and use velcro, so they are easy to fix and don't require pins. Automatic washing machines take most of the effort out of using washable nappies. It's cheaper than using disposables and great for waste prevention.

Even easier is a nappy washing service. You can have dirty nappies collected and freshly laundered ones delivered to your door. Although this costs more to the individual, (at maximum efficiency) a nappy service is easier on the environment than home washing.

Bloody periods!

Sanitary towels and tampons are reasonably visible items in our society. They are advertised on television and in magazines and sold on shop shelves (not under the counter!). But, having said that, we are forever being told that we should cover up the fact that we are menstruating. If we're wearing sanitary protection (sanpro) it must be invisible and, if we're carrying it, it's got to be disguised in zany coloured packages. Advertisers tell us that not only will nobody else know that we are bleeding, but we won't even know ourselves! It's all an attempt at a big cover up. But why? All of us want comfortable and effective sanitary protection but not all of us feel it either necessary or desirable to pretend that the blood doesn't exist.

In some societies the transformation from girlhood to womanhood is marked by special ceremonies and celebration. This isn't usually the case in contemporary British culture. The beginning of menstruation (known as menarche) delivers every girl to the beginnings of womanhood and illustrates her capacity to reproduce. This could be a special time for girls to share with their mothers and other female relatives and friends, but often it is a somewhat embarrassing event which is neither discussed in any detail nor used to make girls feel positive about the changes that are taking place.

In line with the sentiment that bleeding is something we should cover up, until recently we have been encouraged to flush away sanpro even though this is not a suitable disposal route. Flushing quickly removes the 'evidence' but causes problems later when pipes get blocked and beaches and seas get littered with used sanpro – yuck!

Thankfully the Bag It and Bin It campaign has been greeted with support and responsible action on the part of most manufacturers. The 'don't flush it' message is now clearly stated on most packaging and a change in attitudes and practise is taking place.

You can avoid the bin altogether by buying the latest in reusable sanpro. It may not be quite as convenient as the disposable kind but it has other benefits. It can help us to acknowledge menstruation, and regard it as a positive aspect of our lives as well as reducing our use of resources.

Rinsing out cotton towels is fairly straightforward at home in the privacy of your own bathroom – doing it at school or in public toilets could take some bravery! But remember that changes you make in your life don't have to be all or nothing. Even if you only avoided disposables for one day per period think how much paper (and rubbish) you would have saved after a couple of years? Every little action really does help!

What you can do
- Celebrate your femaleness. The fact that the word 'menarche' which describes the first bleed, is absent from both of my dictionaries gives an indication of the value which is attached to this experience by our society. If you think this is an occasion worth celebrating, then have a Bloody Party!
- Complain! It is possible to produce comfortable, biodegradable sanitary towels. If the brand you use contains plastic (which won't biodegrade) you as a consumer can put pressure on manufacturers by writing letters explaining what you want. You might

boycott the product until changes are made. The prospect of losing custom is taken very seriously by manufacturers. So come on, pens at the ready. We want safe, comfortable, affordable, biodegradable sanitary protection – please!

> **Campaigning works!**
> In the late 1980s the Women's Environmental Network exposed the fact that disposable sanpro and similar paper-pulp products contained traces of highly poisonous dioxins. The aim of the campaign was to persuade manufacturers not to use chlorine bleached pulp because it was the bleaching process that produced these dangerous by-products. The publicity highlighted the issue and almost overnight the manufacturers switched to using non-chlorine bleached pulp for these items.
>
> And the moral of the story is: never feel that you, as just one person, have no power to change the behaviour of big companies. Manufacturers are only in business because of their customers – they will listen to you. They probably won't change much on the strength of one letter – but remember that all those single letters add up, and that's when they will start changing. That's why it's so important to complain when you think things aren't right!

- Try reusable sanpro (see Resources). If it's too expensive try making your own (contact WEN).

Using Things Up

It isn't just what we buy that determines how much rubbish we make, but the way that we use things. To be efficient we need to get the maximum use out of the things that we make and buy. We can do this by sharing things with friends and neighbours, by lending things out and by selling on or giving away things that we no longer use but are still useful.

If designers and manufacturers produce goods that will last and can be repaired, this will support a more sharing attitude towards possessions and more efficient use of resources.

Chapter 3

Recycling

Over the past 20 years an infrastructure has developed to enable us, the public, to participate in the collection of materials for recycling. Banks for glass, metal, paper and textiles are familiar to us all. But what's it all about? This chapter will explain the What? Why? and How? of recycling!

A virtuous circle

Recycling specifically means reprocessing materials so that they can be used again. Often wider and more vague interpretations are given which include other activities like reuse and composting, but I'm sticking to a precise definition in this book to avoid confusion. The word 'recycling' describes itself perfectly. Recycling sends materials round in circles. We're familiar with the term 'vicious circle', but living sustainably is all about creating 'virtuous circles'. Recycling is a great example and it's easy to visualise the benefits.

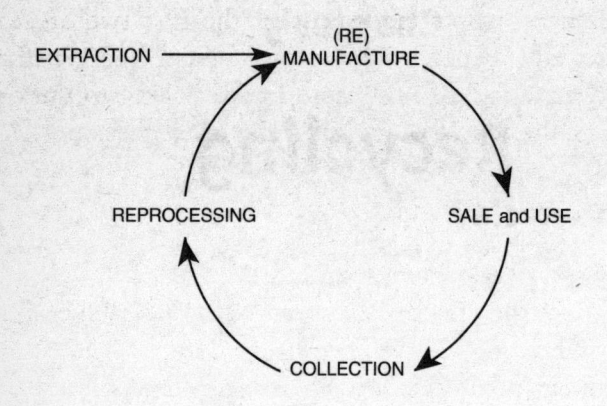

```
EXTRACTION ──────▶ (RE)MANUFACTURE
         ▲              │
         │              ▼
   REPROCESSING     SALE and USE
         ▲              │
         └── COLLECTION ◀┘
```

Definitions

- A beer bottle is recycled when the glass is crushed, melted down and moulded into a new bottle.
- When a beer bottle is refilled, it is being reused, not recycled.
- When a bottle is reprocessed and made into something different which won't be recycled (eg an ornament), this is called 'downcycling'.
- Recycling is about prolonging the useful life of valuable resources rather than prolonging the life of specific items made from those resources.

The three stages

The three elements to recycling are *collection*, *reprocessing* and *marketing* and each is equally important. What we often think of as recycling is just the collection part because this is the most visible. Collections accumulate at home and then at the local bank. Collected materials are sorted and then transported to reprocessing factories. The third element, marketing, is vital if the first two are to continue and expand. There must be a market for recycled materials, because if no one is willing to use or buy them, the whole process falls flat on its face.

Why Recycle?

- It conserves valuable resources.
- It reduces the disruption caused by land clearance for new mines.
- It reduces pollution, and saves energy and money at the extraction, reprocessing and disposal stages.
- It helps to reduce litter and the volume of rubbish going to landfill or incineration.

Putting recycling in its place – reduce – reuse – recycle

Recycling is always good, but it isn't always best because it does still have an environmental impact. It requires energy and creates some pollution. Recycling is the best option if reduction and reuse aren't appropriate or have been exhausted.

Until recently, recycling has been allowed to represent all that is green and to eclipse other waste saving options. This is partly because recycling allows materials to be collected after they have been thrown away, removing responsibility from consumers to actually reduce the amount of waste they create. This suits big companies that want the flexibility that throwaway packaging offers them. In some instances, recycling has been offered to the public in place of reuse, even though reuse is a far better option when well organised.

We need to make big cuts in our use of materials to reduce pollution, conserve resources and allow developing countries a fair chance to raise standards of living. So we have to use materials with maximum efficiency. Recycling has a big part to play and it must be developed, but we mustn't lose sight of more appropriate solutions where they are applicable.

What Can We Recycle?

A lot of what we recycle is packaging: metal cans, cardboard boxes, glass bottles and jars. But not all of the packaging we use is recyclable. Sustainable packaging for the future needs to be reusable wherever possible and always suitable for recycling or composting at the end of its useful life.

Metals are perfectly suited to recycling because their quality isn't diminished by reprocessing. Other materials are suitable but have limitations. For example, paper – made from the cellulose fibres of trees – can only be recycled five times because the pulping process shortens the fibres and eventually they get too short to fix together.

Pre-consumer v. post-consumer recycling

Lots of recycling goes on out of public view and has done so for decades. This is often internal recycling carried out by manufacturers, reprocessing trimmings, offcuts and other excess. These are ideal for reprocessing because they are uncontaminated and ready sorted. This in-house recycling is dismissed by some as not being true recycling because the materials haven't actually been used and reclaimed. Still, it works to bring what might otherwise be considered rubbish back to life, preventing waste and reducing demand on virgin raw materials in the same way that real recycling does.

However, when you are looking to buy recycled, check the labelling to see whether the product contains 'post-consumer waste'. This means materials which have already been bought, used, collected and reprocessed. Sometimes in-house efficiency is passed off as recycling just to attract the green consumer, when to all intents and purposes the products have been made from virgin materials.

Getting to grips

It's estimated that 50 per cent of household waste is actually recyclable. Unfortunately, at the moment nowhere near that amount is being diverted to recycling. You could take the 50 per cent estimate as a target and see if you can halve the amount of waste your household sends to landfill or incineration each week. If you already recycle – excellent! Keep up the good work and encourage others too.

All local authorities (councils) have a waste recycling plan and a recycling officer who is there to help you. If you have any questions, need information or support with a recycling project, or you feel your area needs more recycling facilities, then contact your local recycling officer either by phone or with a letter. You can find the contact details in your local phone book (listed under the local council), local library (ask a member of staff), or call Waste Watch's WasteLine 020 7253 6266.

Different ways of doing it

As well as being organised by local authorities, recycling facilities may be supplied by independent recycling merchants, charities and nowadays even supermarkets. Different systems operate in different areas. In your area you may find any combination of the following facilities:

- **Bring schemes** – you bring your recyclables and deposit them in recycling banks. These banks aren't usually solitary creatures – they tend to be found in groups which cater for clear, green and brown glass, steel and aluminium cans, paper, occasionally plastic bottles and increasingly common textile banks. Any combination of these containers may be found at a recycling centre. Banks are usually located in central areas of towns and supermarket car parks. This encourages efficiency by reducing the need for people to make a special journey to recycle which, if made by car, would detract from the environmental benefits of recycling.
- Local authorities may also have **civic amenity sites** (dumps) which offer additional recycling facilities for batteries, engine oil, 'white goods' (cookers, fridges etc), books, cardboard, and green (garden) waste as well as depositories for hard-to-dispose-of items like broken furniture and safe CFC extraction from fridges and freezers. Usually a special trip with transport is required.
- Increasingly, local councils are employing **kerbside collections** to recoup recyclables which are placed in coloured sacks or boxes to distinguish them from general household waste. The materials are taken to

local sorting depots, and each material returned to the appropriate recycling plant. This kind of scheme costs more than bring schemes to operate, but recovers more materials.

> **Paving the way!**
> The London Borough of Haringey has implemented a borough wide kerbside collection with a difference. It is the first large scale kerbside scheme in Britain to use 'pedestrian controlled vehicles' for collections. These are battery powered vehicles which use the pavement and so avoid blocking congested urban roads in the way that refuse vehicles do. They are believed to be the most efficient collection system available and other London boroughs intend to use them.

- In some areas of the UK you might be collecting steel without even knowing it. If you don't have can banks for steel, the chances are that the steel content of your rubbish is **magnetically extracted** either after incineration (because it doesn't burn) or at a waste treatment plant or materials recovery facility (MRF) and then sent to the steel industry for reprocessing. Incinerated cans lose their thin coating of tin in the process and may be used directly in the manufacture of new steel. If cans aren't incinerated they can be de-tinned through an electrolytic process, then both tin and steel may be reused.
- **Materials recovery facility** Some authorities (eg Greater Manchester Waste Disposal Authority) send their waste to these facilities where materials are separated out by a series of different processes. The

high revenue of some materials (notably aluminium) makes the financial investment required to build such facilities worthwhile.
- Aluminium may be collected at **cash-for-cans points** where about a penny is paid for each can. This can be a good way to raise funds for schools and charities while spreading the recycling message to all who participate.
- As well as accommodating recycling banks, some **supermarkets** collect plastic bags and aluminium foil in-store.
- **Oxfam** collects aluminium foil for recycling. Also, stamps, coins, air-miles vouchers, cigarette cards and coupons, Co-op, Green Shield and Pink Stamps, petrol coupons and used phonecards are all collected at the shops and sent to Oxfam's specialist stamp and coin department for resale.

Recycling Stories

There is a story for each material that is recycled, of how it is collected, where it goes and what happens to it. Read on for the nitty gritty of what actually happens when the collection trucks deposit their loads at the reprocessing plants.

Paper

> In the UK we consume over 11 million tonnes of paper and board a year. About 35 per cent of the paper we use gets recycled. The average household discards 2–3 kg of newspapers and magazines every week.

Paper is made from cellulose fibre. This can come from a range of sources, including wood, rags, cotton, hemp, grasses and straw. However, 99 per cent of fibres for UK papermaking come from waste paper and wood pulp (59 per cent waste paper, 29 per cent imported, 11 per cent homegrown wood pulp). Only 1 per cent is provided by alternative fibres – there is much scope to develop here.

Recycling paper means less trees need to be cut down. Although trees for paper are grown in 'sustainable' forests and replaced by two or three more seedlings when felled, these are not natural habitats – they are plantations that have replaced natural forests, which were originally cut down for paper, destroying biological diversity and valuable carbon sinks. Recycling paper will guard against more old growth forests being destroyed to make paper. It also saves energy (and associated pollution) in the production process and reduces the amount of waste needing to be disposed of.

The industry's use of waste paper has been increasing since the early 1980s but Britain can and should recycle more, although the paper industry can never achieve a 100 per cent recycling rate because:

- Cellulose fibres get damaged each time they are reprocessed. In order to maintain strength and quality they cannot be used more than five times. So there is always demand for new fibres.
- Some paper has permanent uses, for example books, documents, artworks etc, so these fibres cannot be reclaimed.
- Some paper is destroyed or contaminated in the course of its life rendering it unsuitable for recycling.

Although new fibres are a necessary input to the papermaking process, Britain could reduce reliance on woodpulp imports and really save trees by developing the use of alternative fibres in their place. Straw and hemp are highly suitable options. Straw is a regular by-product of arable farming and hemp is a fast growing crop which could be grown on some of the 'set aside' land that farmers are unable to use because of European agricultural policy. This would generate employment and increase self-reliance.

Paper merchants collect paper, magazines and cardboard from local authority depositories, offices and shops. Mixed paper has to be sorted (or graded) by hand into no less than 11 main groups as different fibres have different qualities and therefore uses. Mixing up all papers would downgrade the quality of the whole batch. Any collection scheme where you are asked to separate different types of paper yourself, adds to the system's efficiency. Merchants sort, bale and then forward paper to the mills where the recycling process (similar to the original papermaking process) takes place.

Paper also contains fillers such as china clay and gums, which can make it smoother, heavier, more glossy etc. Removing these is the first step of reprocessing. Paper is cleaned or 'de-inked' either by washing or flotation.

The washing process involves pulping the paper with lots of water and then straining off contaminants such as staples and sticky tape. This process recovers about 80 per cent of the original fibre.

Flotation involves the same pulping process but less water is needed and surfactant chemicals are added, making a sticky froth on the surface. Air bubbles are blown through the pulp, carrying the ink to the surface. It then sticks to the froth and must be removed before the bubbles break otherwise the ink will sink back to the pulp. This method is used for newspapers and magazines and recovers 90–95 per cent of the original mass although fillers added to the cellulose fibres are not removed as efficiently as in the washing process.

The cleaned pulp is passed through a hydro-pulper which further breaks down the fibres making a mixture known as 'stock', 'stuff' or 'porridge'. Any colourings or fillers are added at this stage. The stock is then transferred to the paper-making machine and any new fibres are added. The machine sprays out the stock onto a belt while water is removed by gravity, rollers or suction. A continuous run of paper is made which passes through huge rollers to squeeze more water out. From this 'wet end' the paper passes to the 'dry end' where heated cylinders dry the paper and give it strength as the fibres bond together. The paper is then ironed to smooth the surface and wound up ready to be made into recycled paper products.

You can support paper recycling by choosing to buy recycled products such as writing paper, envelopes, refill pads, cards, books, toilet paper etc. If you can't find recycled goods in your usual shops ask if the shopkeeper has any intention of stocking recycled alternatives because you would like to buy them! You can also save paper for recycling. If you have a large supply of good quality paper you may find that a waste paper merchant or national paper-collection company will actually pay you for it, or at least collect it for free (check your Yellow Pages or contact your recycling officer). Does your school or college recycle? If not, perhaps you could help to set up a scheme.

> **Local paper for London**
> The BioRegional Development Group are producing local paper for London called Evolve. It's 100 per cent recycled from London waste; it's produced at a mill in Kent and is sold back to Londoners. If you live in London ask your headteacher/principal/employer to buy it – contact BioRegional for a price list.

Tips to remember

- Reuse paper wherever possible – both sides please!
- Keep different grades of paper separate for recycling (high quality white paper, newspapers and magazines, cardboard). It's really important to put the right type of paper in the correct skip or bank. Putting high grade paper in with the cardboard is a waste of good quality fibre, and putting cardboard in with high grade waste could downgrade the quality of the entire load.
- Buy recycled to support recycling and request it if it's not there – remember the power of demand and supply.
- Encourage others to recycle and to buy recycled.

Glass

> In the UK we use over six billion glass containers every year but less than a third of these get recycled.

The main raw materials for glass making (sand, soda ash and limestone) are available in plentiful supply. But there are plenty of good reasons for minimising the amount of new glass that is made.

- Glass manufacture requires energy to extract, transport and process the raw materials into the finished product. The ingredients have to be heated to very high temperatures before they melt and can be used. Manufacture is ideally suited to using scrap glass or 'cullet' as there is no loss of quality and it demands 20 per cent less energy and creates 20 per cent less pollution.
- Raw materials have to be quarried from the landscape, so reducing this demand preserves the quality of the landscape and avoids the waste associated with excavation. Water use is halved when cullet is used.
- Although glass is a fairly harmless material (unless it cuts you) it doesn't break down and rot away. Every year at least 1.5 million tonnes of glass is wasted by going to landfill where it will stay unchanged when with a little effort (from us and our local councils) it could be put back into circulation.
- The collection, cleaning and recycling of used glass provides employment opportunities.

Collection facilities for glass recycling were established as bottle deposits became less common. While it's good news that most of us in Britain can easily participate in glass recycling, the down side is that to some extent recycling has replaced the more efficient option of refilling. Still, it's important that a national infrastructure for glass collection has developed, and there are now over 16,000 bottle-bank sites in Britain.

The glass collected at bottle banks is used to make new jars and bottles. The exact composition of glass is dependent upon its intended use – glass for bottles is not the same as glass for windows or wine glasses. This is why it is important to place only bottles and jars in the banks, and why cullet is used to make more of the same.

Collected glass is kept (colour separated) at local depots until a sufficient quantity has accumulated. Then it's taken to the recycling plant where it gets sorted and crushed. Odd bits such as corks, labels and bottle tops are removed either magnetically or mechanically. Then the cullet is mixed with raw materials and heated in a furnace until molten glass is dropped into moulds and formed into bottles and jars. In Britain an average of 30 per cent cullet is used, but some furnaces can use 80 per cent or more. The new containers are sent to bottlers and packers to be filled and then they are distributed to shops throughout the country.

Although the number of bottle bank sites has increased three fold in the past ten years, in the UK we rank amongst the poorest glass recyclers in Europe, only managing to recover 28 per cent of the glass we consume. Compare this to Switzerland's glowing example of 84 per cent. It is glaringly obvious that we need to be working towards much greater efficiency in our use of glass containers.

Tips to remember

- Rinse bottles and jars before recycling.
- Remove caps, lids and corks so that they don't have to be removed later.
- Put the right colour in the right bank. Blue glass can go in the green bank.
- Don't recycle refillable bottles – reuse them!
- Be considerate. Avoid using banks late at night when they can disturb local residents.
- Always put the right thing in – contaminants hamper

the recycling process and can cause unnecessary waste.

Steel

> All steel products have a 25 per cent recycled content. Steel is 100 per cent recyclable and its magnetic property makes it easy to separate for recycling. Around 300 million tonnes per year is recycled representing a saving on raw materials of approximately 200 million tonnes of iron ore and 90 million tonnes of coal!

Steel is made from iron ore, limestone and recovered steel. The industry is well established and recycling has always been an important part of the business.

In the UK we use 13 billion steel cans each year, but we only recycle about about 15 per cent of these (2 billion cans). However, in areas where local authorities use magnetic extraction to collect steel the rates are more like 80 per cent. We should strive for a national recycling rate much nearer to this figure because although rates are on the increase they are still low compared to many other European countries. It would also mean we'd make bigger savings on energy and raw materials than we presently do. Magnetic extraction can recover all steel items, not just cans. One waste disposal authority estimated that magnetic extraction saved £2000 each week on waste disposal.

> A 1990 Swiss study showed that a steel can with ring pull consumed one third less energy than PET plastic bottles and one quarter less than PVC and non-returnable glass.

An even larger source of scrap steel is old cars and other vehicles. More than half of the average car is steel and this can be recovered at the end of the vehicle's life. This is a well established business which feeds the steel industry. Breakers yards or scrap-car dealers are also reuse businesses which strip all the useful bits from vehicles and sell them to the public providing a cheap alternative to buying new parts, reusing items that are often not recyclable.

Civic amenity sites usually have facilities for collecting scrap metal which is then sold on to scrap metal merchants and recycled.

Most of us get involved with steel recycling by saving food and drinks cans. Often aluminium and steel are collected together. Cans are taken to regional depots where they are sorted into steel and aluminium. When sufficient steel cans have been collected for efficient transportation they go to a processing plant where they are shredded and contaminants removed. The metal is then cleaned and de-tinned using chemicals. Then both the tin and steel are washed and sent for recycling.

At the steelworks the scrap is fed into a large furnace (or converter) along with molten iron. The converter is heated to about 2000°C and oxygen is blown onto the metal to remove impurities. The hot steel is poured out and cast into slabs and rolled into coils then dispatched to producers of steel products, such as can makers.

Tips to remember

- If your local council magnetically sorts steel cans from your waste you don't need to separate them out. If this is the case, you probably won't have can banks anyway.
- Rinse and crush your cans before depositing.

- You can put aerosol cans in can banks but they must be empty and *must not be crushed*!
- If you need to separate steel and aluminium cans use a magnet against the side of the can – not the top because some steel drinks cans have aluminium ring-pull tops. Aluminium isn't magnetic.
- Anyone with large steel objects to dispose of can contact a recycling officer or a local scrap merchant so that they can either be reused or recycled.

Aluminium

> - Recycling aluminium requires 90–95 per cent less energy than production from ore (bauxite), and produces 99 per cent less emissions!
> - About a quarter of all aluminium produced in the UK (60,000 tonnes) is used to make drink cans, about 5.5 billion of them every year. About one third are currently recycled. Plenty of room for improvement!

Aluminium recycling is especially important because its creation is particularly energy intensive and polluting. Aluminium is produced from bauxite which is typically mined, processed and smelted in rainforest regions. This involves the destruction of areas of rainforest and associated problems – not least the displacement from their homes of indigenous peoples, who often suffer insult in addition to injury when sites sacred to them are desecrated.

The processing of bauxite into usable aluminium demands enormous amounts of electricity. Alumina powder is extracted then turned into a metal by an electrolytic process (passing a powerful electric current through melted minerals). Polluting by-products such as fluoride are produced which can harm workers, local inhabitants and the wider environment.

Aluminium is easy to recycle – there is no loss of quality and therefore no limit to the number of times that it can be reprocessed. It's commercially viable because of the high market value and the fact that there is a guaranteed market (the Aluminium Can Recycling Association (ACRA) has undertaken to maintain an attractive price). Anyone can make money by returning aluminium cans to a buy-back scheme or other dealer. Can collection is a favoured fundraising activity by schools.

Aluminium cans represent around 2 per cent of domestic waste but account for over 50 per cent of the value of a given mix of recyclables. Local authorities often find the cost of collecting and sorting recyclables from waste prohibitively expensive and use revenues from aluminium to subsidise recycling of other lower value materials.

Clean aluminium foil (from milk bottle tops, takeaway containers and sweet papers etc) can also be collected for recycling and, like cans, also has fundraising potential. Foil has to be collected separately from cans because it is made from a different alloy. Your recycling officer should be able to tell you if you have a local scheme in operation. If not, Oxfam shops will take it (and raise money from it) and the Aluminium Foil Recycling Association can provide further information. Collecting and washing little bits of foil can be fiddly and time consuming, but it takes up less space than other recyclables and represents true dedication to recycling!

Cans are collected at regional depots, then, when sufficient cans have been collected they are taken to

Alcan's aluminium can recycling plant in Warrington, Cheshire. This has been in operation since 1991 and has the capacity to recycle 60,000 tonnes of aluminium each year. The aluminium portion of steel cans is recovered at the de-tinning plant and sent back to the aluminium industry for recycling.

Cans are shredded and de-coated of paint before being melted and cast into huge ingots that weigh 26 tonnes! Each of these ingots represents nearly 1.5 million cans! The ingots go to a rolling mill where they are rolled into sheets and then made into new cans. This is called 'closed loop recycling', where used products are reprocessed to make more of the same product.

Cans are straightforward – they contain easily separated materials, have an established infrastructure for collection and can be economically recycled back into cans. But what of the aluminium that serves different purposes?

What about the aluminium that lines the paper cartons of fruit juice and milk of which we're all now so familiar? It is technically possible to recycle them but it's neither simple nor economic so it doesn't happen. Perhaps we should be getting back to the bottle!

The aluminium in domestic appliances and electronic equipment more often than not goes to waste because there aren't facilities available to recover it. There are employment opportunities in the dismantling and recycling element of the waste industry. If the aluminium industry injected the same enthusiasm into recycling the 180,000 tonnes of aluminium produced in the UK which is not made into cans, as it reserves for beverage cans, then we could really see a difference to our recycling achievements.

Tips to remember
- Don't chuck your drink cans in the bin. Save them for the can bank.
- The value of aluminium makes a can collection an ideal fundraiser. You could organise a collection at school. Cans take up space, so you might suggest your school invests in a can crusher with the first proceeds!

Textiles

> - It's estimated that we annually discard between half a million and a million tonnes of textiles from our homes and it is thought that only about one quarter of this is recovered.
> - Recycling textiles reduces the impact of chemicals used to grow raw materials like cotton, and reduces the consumption of oil used to make synthetic fibres.
> - Dangerous chemicals are used to treat and dye textiles – these can be reduced by maximising the useful life of materials and re-manufacturing when appropriate.
> - Resale and recycling of textiles raises money for charities and provides employment for merchants.

Textile recycling in Britain is a long established industry which, despite its environmental credentials, has a very low profile. In less affluent times we got maximum use out of our clothes and other textiles (curtains and sheeting) and when they were worn out the rag and bone man would collect them up and sell them on for re-manufacture. This kind of system indicates a community and individuals that valued materials in a way that few of us do today, now that as a nation we have become more prosperous. It's common for us to discard clothes simply because we're bored with them or they've gone out of fashion.

Rag and bone men may now be few and far between, but the charity sector has stepped in to maximise the value of the textiles that we discard. The first priority of charity shops is to resell, but textiles that are too worn to sell to the public get sold on to merchants for recycling.

Oxfam has its own waste-saver plant which processes about 80 tonnes of used clothing a week! Most of this comes from Oxfam shops. Unwearable textiles still have useful fibres that have outlived their first incarnation. These take different paths depending on what they are made from.

- Woollen garments are colour sorted and sold to specialist firms where the fibres are shredded to make 'shoddy', then carded and spun into yarn again or made into fabric.
- Rags are sold to the 'filling and flock' industry. They are shredded to be used as fillers in car insulation, roofing felts, loudspeaker cones, panel linings, furniture padding etc.
- Cotton and silk items are graded and some are used to make cleaning cloths for a range of industries and some are used to make specialist papers.

Textile banks have now joined the ranks of other recycling depositories in car parks and civic amenity sites. This adds convenience, as well as helping to raise public awareness of textile recycling and its environmental as well as social benefits.

Tips to remember

- Donate unwanted textiles to charity shops or textile banks.

- Buy second hand, it's fun and you never know what wonders you might end up taking home. You could benefit a charity, the environment and your wardrobe at the same time.
- If you are feeling creative, design your own clothes and then scour jumble sales for cheap material, in the guise of old clothes, and use it to make your own unique apparel.
- Buy recycled if you can. Clothes made from recycled fibres aren't widely available nor particularly cheap, but they are being made and support for this sector will make it grow. Contact WasteWatch for details. Look out for recycled fleeces made from old plastic bottles!

Plastic

> In the UK we consume about 4 million tonnes of plastic every year and discard nearly 2.5 million tonnes, most of it in domestic waste – short-life packaging like food containers and wrappings. Only about 5 per cent of used plastic waste is currently recycled – that includes commercial, industrial and domestic waste.

The plastics industry is very new compared to the other materials industries we've looked at, and plastic recycling is even newer. Plastics are made primarily from oil and natural gas. They are based on long molecules called polymers. Recycling theoretically conserves valuable raw materials and reduces the energy requirement in processing but plastic recycling is a controversial subject and many environmentalists oppose it. So what's the problem?

Recycling light plastics may not actually conserve

resources. It may take as much, or more energy (ie oil) to transport them for recycling, as it would to use new oil to make new plastic. Also, plastics tend to be downcycled rather than recycled (for example, into garden furniture, fibre-fill duvets or fleece jackets). This means that there is not a continuous, closed loop whereby an item is made, used, and reprocessed back into the same thing – for example, a drinks bottle or a yoghurt pot. This is mainly for hygiene reasons. There are stringent controls on the quality of packaging materials that come into contact with foodstuffs (and rightly so), but although the technology does exist to produce food-safe recycled packaging it is not widely available.

There is a downcycling scheme called Save-A-Cup for polystyrene cups used in drinks vending machines. The scheme is aimed at the office workplace where cups are flaked on site and collected when new cups are delivered. The flakes get processed into office accessories, video cassettes, vending cup holders and vending machine components. It's certainly an improvement on 'chuck-a-cup', but I want to know why the trusty mug has been deemed unsuitable for office use. Surely the best way to 'save-a-cup' is to use it over and over again. (And it's certainly nicer to drink out of!)

Considering the low rate of plastic recycling, the amount of energy this process uses and the fact that the plastics that are just discarded don't rot, there is a concern that plastics are being used inappropriately, for purposes equally suited to other materials that are easier to recycle or biodegrade.

Environmentalists have promoted the use of reusable shopping bags in favour of plastic throwaways and, to give them their due, the larger supermarkets have made a lot of progress in reducing shopping-bag waste. Sainsbury's offer a penny back for every bag of theirs you don't use. Not a huge incentive, but the message is spot on. Tesco, Waitrose and Sainsbury's now offer the 'bag for life' – a strong plastic bag that costs 10p. When the bag breaks you take it back and exchange it for a new one at no extra cost and the old one gets reprocessed into plastic benches for weary shoppers! Safeway collect plastic bags and reprocess them too. It's still probably better to take your own bag or rucksack, but the value of these schemes comes in reminding us of the value of resources.

There are about 50 family groups of plastics and even more different varieties. This is one of the reasons that plastic recycling has been slow to develop. If plastics are not source separated then it has to be done later, requiring expensive machinery and energy. A marking code has been developed to help people identify the six main types of plastic that are used in packaging. However, this is only useful if local collection facilities refer to the same code and explicitly state what types of plastic can be deposited. Inadequate information can lead to confusion.

It's a while since I saw a piece of plastic packaging that *didn't* have the recyclable symbol on it – from plastic bottles to food cartons and the clingfilm they are wrapped in. Unfortunately there is a huge gulf between what is possible in theory and what is happening in practice. The bottom line with plastics is that most local authorities don't collect them at all, and those that do only collect plastic bottles. The vast majority of plastic packaging goes in the bin – despite the fact that the little symbol says it is recyclable.

There are a number of plastic recycling schemes in operation in Britain and some of them do actually recycle rather than downcycle. For example Dunlop have a scheme where they recycle wellington boots back into wellington boots. Other companies are recycling clothes hangers and car bumpers, but such initiatives are not given adequate publicity. Considering we live in an age of such advanced communications we should know where and how to do the right thing with our waste. After all, we are bombarded with information on where and how to *buy* things.

Tips to remember

- Plastic recycling is in its infancy. If we are going to continue using so much plastic packaging then it needs a speedy development. Lobby companies that use plastic packaging – try sending it back to them!
- If you don't have plastic recycling facilities try to avoid those products that create plastic waste.

The Next Move

Recycling needs to develop as current recycling initiatives focus mainly on packaging. As well as increasing the volume of recycling through these initiatives, we need to widen the scope of recycling to include a greater diversity of items. What we are lacking is an infrastructure for dismantling and recycling longer life products which are made from many different, and often valuable, materials.

Old goods need new opportunities

Our homes harbour an ever increasing number of consumer durables – computers, televisions, videos, toasters, kettles, vacuum cleaners, microwaves, fridges, freezers, washing machines, the list goes on. When these wear out, get damaged beyond repair or, in the case of computers, become obsolete they still usually contain a number of valuable materials, but there are limited facilities available to make use of them.

Dismantling such items is labour intensive and could therefore create jobs. Parts could be saved for reuse where possible or collected for recycling. This would build on and extend an existing network of second-hand and scrap dealers earning a living in Britain already. Car breakers have an established history of providing a second-hand parts service and steel recycling, although a 'motor vehicle graveyard' is probably the last thing that pops into your head when you think 'recycling'. The low status scrap trade needs reviving, updating and giving greater public profile as a green industry. Local authorities can help by publicising these resource-conscious, waste saving businesses. Keep on recycling those bottles and cans, but to really make some headway in preserving our resources there is much more we can do.

Keeping it local

Some of the benefits of recycling are lost when materials have to travel long distances by road in order to be reprocessed. The ideal scenario is for us to develop fairly small-scale local recycling factories that are well organised and provide decently paid work for local people.

The BioRegional Development Group is working to create a model paper cycle that is both sustainable and local for the production of fine quality papers. The project aims to produce local paper with the participation of local businesses. Companies will save their waste paper to be collected for recycling and upgrading (with locally derived agricultural pulp – not trees) at a 'minimill' and then the paper will be sold back to the same companies, creating a perfect recycling loop.

Keeping it clean

We could reduce road haulage and associated pollution by transferring some cargoes to our under-used system of waterways. We could make greater use of our rivers and reinvent the canal network with 'bottle barges' and 'paper boats'!

Stimulating recycling

Many countries throughout the world (and 11 US States) have deposit legislation to promote the recycling of drinks containers. Throughout the world, giving a financial incentive for customers to return recyclable packaging corresponds with high rates of recycling. We don't have deposit legislation in Britain, although in June 1998 Christopher Leslie, MP for Shipley, launched a private member's bill calling for five pence deposits to be paid by consumers on all bottles and cans. The bill didn't have government backing and it wasn't enacted. The Department of the Environment, Transport and the Regions are hopeful that the packaging regulations alone will work to stimulate recycling.

Where retailers are bound by deposit legislation they need to find ways of efficiently reimbursing consumers and collecting and storing returned containers. The reverse vending machine has been designed and marketed for this purpose. A reverse vending machine will accept an empty beverage container (glass, metal or plastic with a different machine for each material) and then return a coin or voucher as payment. There are in fact some such machines in operation in Britain – they are currently part of a pilot project being conducted in two Somerfield stores in the West of England. Somerfield are using the machines to help meet their packaging waste obligations and to increase customer loyalty, as the vending machines give customer loyalty points rather than hard cash.

Buying recycled

We've already mentioned the importance of having a market for recycled goods. This stage of the process is just as important as collection, although until recently it has been neglected. To boost the market for recycled goods we need greater on-product information detailing recycled content and more general publicity.

To some people, the term 'recycled' seems to have connotations of poor quality and second best, and they will actively avoid recycled products because they think that they are inferior. It's important to get away from the idea that recycling and the careful use of resources is a poor person's/nation's option; bestowing greater value and appreciation on the resources we use will enhance and enrich our lives in the short, medium and long term. Let's do it!

The Local Authority Recycling Advisory Committee (LARAC) now has a Buy Recycled Campaign, which targets the general public through local authority recycling officers and aims to educate and inform people of the merits of recycling and quality of recycled goods. You may have seen the Buy Recycled logo around. The campaign aims to:

- encourage public participation and support for recycling schemes
- raise public awareness of recycled products and packaging with recycled content
- provide information on the availability and quality of recycled products and packaging in order to stimulate markets
- close the recycling loop using the campaign slogan: 'Buy It, Recycle It, Buy Recycled'.

If you want to find out more about recycled products ask your local recycling officer.

What you can do
- Investigate the recycling opportunities available in your area by contacting your local council's recycling officer.
- Use your local recycling facilities.
- Use the Resources section to find out more information.
- Encourage others to participate in recycling.
- Choose to buy products made from recyclable materials and let manufacturers and retailers know that you support recycled products.
- Make your own recycled paper.
- Establish a recycling scheme at your school or college.
- Reduce the need for recycling by rejecting excess packaging and junk mail, and by reusing and refilling wherever possible.

Chapter 4

Working Waste

Some of the waste we produce can neither be avoided, reused (for its original purpose), nor recycled. But that doesn't mean we have to throw it away! There are some types of waste that can be set to work again. Far from being redundant, they can be highly productive.

Home Composting

Composting is sometimes referred to as recycling. But rather than reprocessing materials (eg paper back into paper, glass back into glass), composting involves a transformation of materials. Food scraps and plant trimmings are transformed into soil conditioner. This can be used to help to grow more food and garden plants to complete a cyclical process. The materials follow a circular route, but it's not, perhaps, as obvious as the loop that's created by recycling.

Food scraps and garden trimmings have very limited uses in their current form. You may have a pet that polishes off some of your vegetable trimmings or leftovers and keen gardeners might use grass cuttings for mulch (ground cover to prevent drying), but then again you may not have a pet or be a keen gardener! Many people don't have 'working' gardens, and they associate composting with their green-fingered friends. But you don't have to be a slave to the garden to be a composter. This is a really satisfying form of waste prevention because you're not just diverting stuff out of the bin – in a totally natural way you're actually making a whole new resource!

Composting is an excellent way to reduce waste on a daily basis. It doesn't require any major changes or take up much time in your life. You will be reducing the amount of stuff you put in the dustbin by putting it in the compost bin instead. You should notice the difference immediately because about a quarter of what we throw away each week is compostable material.

Local councils have no obligation to remove garden waste such as lawn mowings and plant trimmings. Householders may have to pay to have this type of waste taken away. So composting can save money too, or at least a trip to the civic amenity site. Gardeners value compost because it nourishes and enriches the soil. For others, it reduces waste and avoids a smelly dustbin full of rotting food scraps. Composting can be a first step in raising people's consciousness to the wider issues of waste and the environment.

Getting started

If you are going to compost you'll need:

- a compost bin!
- a garden with enough space to put it (a sunny spot is best)
- an area to add the finished compost to (unless you're going to give it away)
- a bucket or bowl to collect waste in the kitchen.

Councils often subsidise compost bins because it saves them money when residents compost. On top of the basic cost of disposal (about £20 per tonne), since the introduction of the Landfill Tax it costs councils an additional £11 per tonne to deposit waste in landfill sites. So in areas where rubbish goes to landfill, councils make a double saving when you compost.

Check out the price of bins in a local garden centre, then contact your local council's recycling officer to find out what sort of a deal they can offer – you can impress your parents with your research and they'll probably be bowled over by the kind of discounts some councils are offering! If you're short of time, go straight to the council. If your folks need convincing that the outlay on a compost bin is worth it, you could remind them that the less the council has to pay in disposal costs, the less they will have to levy through the council tax!

Alternatively you might like to build your own. Helpful information on how to do this is available from Wyecycle and other organisations listed in the Resources section. One of the simplest ways is to stack up worn-out tyres. Check out local garages for possible freebies.

What can you use?

Anything biodegradable can be composted. You can compost all your fruit and veg. peelings, scraps of food, egg shells, tissue paper, torn up newspaper that can't be recycled because it's soiled, egg boxes, loo-roll tubes, cotton wool, tea leaves and bags, coffee grounds, sawdust and lawn mowings in small quantities.

Tumble-dryer fluff and vacuum-cleaner contents can be used, but the fluff will only rot if it comes from natural fibres. If your carpets and clothes are mainly synthetic, avoid composting this fluff. It's generally recommended that you don't compost meat or cooked foods at home because it might attract rats.

You can collect your compostables in a bowl or bucket in the kitchen and then empty it into the bin every day or so, depending on how much you produce and what the weather is like. (You won't want scraps hanging around very long in the summer when it's hot because they will attract flies and start to smell really quickly! A bucket with a lid is ideal.)

Make it 50:50
The Centre for Alternative Technology's recipe for perfect, no-fuss compost is a mix of 50 per cent foodstuff with 50 per cent paper and card. If you just add food to your bin not enough air can circulate, it gets slimy and – to be blunt – it stinks! But if you add a good mix of paper and cardboard items and make sure that they are torn up or scrunched up as appropriate, the air can pass through, speeding up rotting and producing a fine product that requires very little maintenance. Just be sure that the paper and food are reasonably well mixed.

Fallen leaves and woody prunings rot quite slowly so these should be heaped up separately or added to the green waste skip at your local dump (this will get composted). Adding them to your compost bin at home in large quantities will fill it very quickly and slow the composting process right down. In any case a pile of leaves at the end of the garden is good for wildlife, including hedgehogs looking for a winter hideout!

> **Hedgehog awareness!**
> If you do leave a heap of leaves and prunings in your garden do be aware that hedgehogs might take refuge in the autumn and winter months – so don't go and pile them all on a bonfire or go at them with a pitchfork if you want to clear them away!

The science of it

Composting is a way of speeding up the natural process of organic decomposition (in this context 'organic' is used as a general term that includes all plant based materials). Organic matter is placed in a confined space, with air allowed to circulate. Bacteria breeds and breaks down the material. The end product is compost, and carbon dioxide is produced as a by-product. If the process is working properly the temperature will rise high enough to kill the seeds of weeds and destroy harmful bacteria (pathogens).

The contents of a bin will take somewhere between three months and a year to fully rot. The final product should be dry and crumbly. Composting isn't difficult but you do need to keep an eye on it to make sure it's working reasonably efficiently – if the process is going too slowly you'll end up with a full bin and no finished compost to remove to make space for your constant stream of organic waste!

The process has been likened to cooking, in that you need to have the right balance of ingredients (including air and heat) in order for the mixture to cook properly. The great thing about compost though is that you can't overcook it! It never really goes wrong, if the mix of ingredients aren't quite right you can address the problem by adding more of what is needed to speed the process along. If you think your compost isn't working properly, or it smells horrid or is attracting flies, plenty of good advice is available from composting organisations and the Centre for Alternative Technology.

If you have one bin, you can lift it up, or open a flap if it has one, and remove the finished compost at the bottom and continue to fill it at the top. If you're quite a big household and produce a lot of waste, two bins are a good idea if you have the space. This way you can fill one and leave it to finish while filling the second. By the time you've topped up number two the first one should be ready to empty completely and then you can start to refill it.

> **Hot tip!**
> If you line your compost bin with a few sheets of newspaper or thin cardboard it saves the bin getting grotty and makes it a lot easier to empty!

Working Worms!

A slightly different slant on composting is 'vermiculture'. This is where worms transform food scraps into garden fertiliser. The worms live in a wormery which you can keep either indoors or outside. It doesn't take up as much space as a compost bin and you don't need a garden. You need to remove the compost and drain off the liquid they produce as and when necessary.

You add your kitchen waste and the worms will break it down by eating, digesting and excreting it and the result is excellent garden fertiliser. If you don't have your own garden you can use it for window boxes or give it to a friend. Worms alone can't deal with the same sort of quantity or variety of input that a compost bin can, although they might be more fun. Consider your needs when deciding what to go for and if in doubt seek some expert advice (see Resources).

The worms you need are brandling worms or tiger worms (rather than earthworms). You'll probably have to buy them specially, because you will only find them where they have a plentiful supply of food. You can get them from fishing-tackle shops (and the worms might appreciate a life of munching fruit and veg. instead of being eaten by fish!). They are thin, dark red worms, easily distinguished from the plump, pink earthworms.

When going on holiday you'll have to make sure they've got enough food. If you're away for more than a couple of days, get a friend to provide fresh trimmings. If you need to disband your wormery, find a friend or neighbour with a compost bin – they'll be delighted to welcome your worms.

If you have a compost bin you may find brandling worms already in there feeding on the contents. This is a great bonus because the worms keep decomposition going all year round, even when it gets colder in the winter and the action of the bacteria slows down or stops altogether.

Community Composting

Community composting schemes are developing throughout Britain. Some are run by local councils as part of their efforts to reduce waste going to landfill (and to meet government targets to recover value from 40 per cent of municipal waste by 2005). Other projects are independent, local, business ventures (for example Wyecycle, see page 61) or waste minimisation projects (like the Old Spitalfields Market project).

These projects collect and/or receive organic waste from householders, shops, market traders, cafes and restaurants and turn it into top quality compost which can be used by local farmers or bagged up and sold back to the local community. This a great example of getting the most out of our waste and using it to generate employment and money in an environmentally sustainable way. There is the environmental impact of transportation, which doesn't apply to home composting, but these are local projects so travelling distances are kept to a minimum and they may use pedal or battery powered vehicles to further reduce pollution.

At Old Spitalfields Market in London the waste minimisation project initiated by the Women's Environmental Network involves collecting and transporting food waste from the market to the local Hackney City Farm where some of it is used as animal feed and the rest of it for composting. It travels via the Green Goddess – an old battery powered milk float!

Local food production

The compost produced at the City Farm helps to support a local food production business, the Coriander Club. Local Bangladeshi women use the compost and space at the City Farm to grow herbs (notably coriander!) which are then sold at Old Spitalfields Market for local consumption.

An organic vegetable box scheme in North London – 'Growing Communities' – distributes organic food (as you would expect!) but it is also developing local growing sites with the aim of producing locally grown organic food for local people (in this case, 'organic' means food grown without the use of chemical pesticides and fertilisers). Beyond this the growing sites provide an opportunity for city dwellers not only to buy local organic food, but to actually grow it themselves. The sites also enable small-scale community composting.

Linking up with agriculture

Some experimental community composting schemes in the West of England are putting waste to work in agriculture. Householders separate their plant-based waste and it is collected and taken to a nearby organic farmer who composts the material on his land and uses the end product on his farm.

The projects have been carefully thought out and the results have been very positive. The compost produced has very low levels of physical contamination (non-biodegradable bits like plastic), a good balance of nutrients and meets the standards required for use on organic farms.

Connecting food waste with food production is an efficient and sustainable way of managing our waste. If you live on an arable farm and could make use of large amounts of household organic waste, why not contact your local recycling officer to discuss the possibilities?

Setting up schemes at school or college

Schools and colleges could deal with waste on site by composting food waste and shredded paper to produce soil conditioner for the grounds. Busy canteens ensure a regular supply of food scraps and could be ideal places to set up wormeries or composting schemes. It may not be possible to deal with all food waste this way. Meat waste should be separated out to avoid problems with rats.

You may be able to contribute to a community composting scheme, or help to establish a new one. Talk to your teachers, your local recycling officer and contact the Community Composting Network for support and advice.

Setting up a project in school means you can see composting in action. There are lots of different educational angles, so prepare your case and take it to your teachers or lecturers. It also provides a positive example to everybody of how to deal with waste responsibly.

Composting: the benefits
- takes messy waste out of the bin, avoiding contamination of other items which could be sorted and recovered for recycling after collection
- reduces rubbish going to landfill or incineration
- an easy step to a more sustainable lifestyle
- makes valuable soil improver which builds up long-term soil structure and fertility
- saves buying peat or compost for the garden, and so
- preserves the fragile environments of peat bogs

Waste Paper!

Composting may be the most familiar example, but it's not the only way to get waste working again!

We've already discussed the fact that paper recycling has its limitations ie after four or five times the cellulose fibres are too short to do the job properly. So, there will always be a need for new fibre input in paper making. Trees aren't the only plant that can provide cellulose fibres. Non-tree paper can be made from a variety of fibre sources.

Straw that is left after grain crops have been harvested can be used for paper making. Farmers used to burn it off, but this is no longer allowed. Using it as a raw material in paper making gives it a new lease of life, not to mention economic value. Straw fibres are not of the highest quality because they are fairly short, but the shortcomings of straw can be compensated for by the addition of hemp, which offers the finest quality fibres. Hemp is a fast growing multifunctional plant which has a seemingly endless number of applications. However, in its role in paper making, it can be added to a mix of straw and old paper to upgrade the quality of recycled paper.

The BioRegional Development Group has been instrumental in designing a minimill to produce non-wood paper (eg straw–hemp–recycled paper). The idea is to produce paper from local sources that can then be sold locally. The input of 'new' fibres required can be supplied by straw that would otherwise be a waste product and hemp which can be grown cheaply, easily and sustainably. This reduces the need to fell trees for paper as well as reducing our dependence (and expenditure) on imported materials. Check out the BioRegional web site for more information about their projects.

Chapter 5

The Way Ahead

It's easy to feel gloomy and pessimistic about the future of our planet. News and current-affairs programmes often bring stories of environmental disasters. Environmentalists and concerned scientists make programmes to try to change the behaviour of big corporations and governments. It's important that environmental issues are discussed in the media. But often the message that this conveys is one of doom and gloom because they do not highlight the power *we* have. It simply isn't true that everything we are doing at the moment is bad for the planet. There are so many projects and even more people out there aiming towards sustainable lifestyles. Through science and technology we are gaining more understanding about the way nature works and how humans can benefit from working with, rather than against nature. The future is full of possibility. There are amazing ways for the human race to develop — we just need to make it happen by supporting sustainable initiatives and showing the people who hold power the kind of future we want.

We can focus on preventing waste by truly valuing the materials we use and the products we make with them. By doing this we will use resources more efficiently. We won't have to argue about the best way to get rid of our waste if we don't make the rubbish in the first place. Ideally all the surplus produced by a society would either be reusable, recyclable or compostable. We need to eliminate 'rubbish' as a concept and let our vision take us beyond the bin.

Change Your Own Mind

Wanting to live a low waste lifestyle and actually doing it are not the same thing. There is huge pressure from large companies who employ expensive advertising companies to persuade us that we need all manner of things. Television, radio and billboards are constantly exposing us to ever more products in ever wackier packaging. It's extremely difficult to remain unaffected by the constant barrage of advertising slogans, and peer pressure doesn't help.

Women and girls are placed under particular pressures by consumer society to look and behave in certain ways. We are given representations to aspire to (body image, fashion, make-up etc), and it is rarely suggested that we question the values of that society. But we may feel destined to aspire to something altogether different and what then? We should feel comfortable to be ourselves, however we see ourselves, and we should feel free to follow our own dreams. It can often be difficult to determine what we personally want as opposed to what we are expected to want or what manufacturers want us to buy. For example, do you wear make-up? Why is that? Are you conforming to social expectations? Do you feel pressure to behave a certain way because you are a woman? Are you rebelling against social expectations? Are you making a political statement? Have you considered the politics of lipstick?! Be whoever you want to be – but it's worth considering the influences that impact on your decision-making.

In spite of these pressures it is brilliant that young people are so clued up about environmental issues and are prepared to stand up in defence of the environment. It is often the younger members of a household that inspire others to think about the consequences of their actions. A recent Co-op survey reported in *The Guardian* that 70 per cent of 15–19 year old women put pressure on their parents to shop ethically. Energy and enthusiasm are catching – it's not necessarily going to be difficult to persuade others to make low waste decisions. Being wasteful doesn't make sense, being resourceful does and it feels good too.

I recently read in a local newspaper about a group of teenagers who had stepped in to save a furniture recycling project from folding. The van that the voluntary project used to collect unwanted furniture needed repairs that the project couldn't afford. The young people organised a sponsored 'stay awake' and raised enough money to keep the van and the project on the road. Their activities also helped to raise the profile of the furniture project, so it gained more customers.

There are all sorts of positive changes you can make in your life. If you don't already do it, I hope you'll start collecting materials for recycling or try composting, or extend your vision even further beyond the bin and think about making lifestyle changes which tackle more subtle forms of waste. For example, shopping for clothes can become a green activity! Consider the following:

- check out the local charity shops
- think about the quality of clothing in terms of how long it will last
- where was it made and who by? Were they paid a decent wage?
- think about future possibilities for recycling when the garment has worn out.

What about food? You're out and about (shopping for recycled paper and a pair of hemp jeans!) and desperate for a bite to eat and something to drink, and you certainly don't have the money for a sit-down meal with proper plates! What can you do to satisfy your hunger and thirst without it costing the Earth? I'm not about to tell you what you can and can't do – that's something you have to decide for yourself! But you might consider a drink in a reusable mug or recyclable container (metal or glass) and something to eat that has minimal packaging – something from the bakers or sandwich shop in, at most, a paper bag – rather than a drink in a one-use plastic cup and a burger in a throwaway styrofoam box.

These are just some of the issues that going shopping can expose. Once you start looking you begin to see waste everywhere – but then you start to see solutions too. We can find ways to save waste in everything we do, but don't let it be a drudge. It should be fun, a challenge and something that makes you feel good because you are taking positive action. We can make other people feel good too by supporting those who are providing waste-saving products and services. Once we have changed our minds about waste, the actions will follow.

No Waste Please

Our challenge is to develop systems through which we can make, sell, buy, and use things so that wherever possible resources cycle around and are used to their fullest capacity. In addition it's important that we have maximum durability and repairability. This challenge is already being met by all sorts of people in all sorts of ways. This chapter aims to inspire you to go ahead and meet the challenge.

Different materials have different potential and different life cycles. A steel can, for instance, will enjoy many incarnations, coming back over and again as a can, but a paper bag will soon tear or become soiled – if it is clean it may be reused or recycled but if it is soiled it can be added to the compost heap where it can transform from a useless paper bag into useful soil conditioner.

It's important to keep in mind where things have come from and where they will go. By thinking about the wider picture, we can make informed decisions about the way we want to live our lives. Once you focus on the big picture, suddenly everything is politicised. What you choose to buy, to eat, and everything else you do has an impact on the world around you. Feeling that truth for yourself is a rite of passage, and it brings both responsibility and power. As individuals we can be a powerful force for change, and when we unite with others we become even stronger.

Individual responsibility is vital. We all need to account for the way we interact with our environment but responsibility must be taken at all levels. Local and national government, small and large businesses, in fact every sector of society should take responsibility for the present and future state of the environment.

Of course waste prevention isn't a new invention. Many waste preventing systems have been around for a very long time. We've already looked at long established recycling industries, and any business that fixes things is preventing waste, from cobblers to car mechanics. Reuse and recycling have been embraced by some businesses because these measures are efficient and economic. They work well and save money. But to achieve sustainable economic development we need to make fundamental changes which reflect a revolution in our attitude towards resources. We need to change as consumers, designers, manufacturers and advertisers. Yes, we need to change our actions and activities, but we also need to change our perception. We need to see things differently, with new vision. By changing our attitude to waste and no longer regarding it as a tolerable (if undesirable) side effect of modern life, we really will be changing the world.

Changing Industry

It is true we have environmental legislation to safeguard people and the planet against some industrial pollution. But laws only set standards that ought to be maintained, they don't provide any guarantees. They are also slow to change. The steady, conservative nature of the law tends to create a generation gap whereby laws reflect the previous generation's view of the world.

The standard attitude of governments is that pollution should be controlled rather than avoided. This is generally done by introducing what are called 'end of pipe' solutions, eg fitting filters to prevent poisonous waste escaping into the air. This simply contains the pollution instead of preventing it. Air quality may have been maintained but poisonous waste still exists and becomes a hazard to soil and water. This type of action exposes the assumption that a certain degree of pollution is acceptable. We need a much more radical response than that! Industrial production is important to the economies of many countries and consequently to the lives of millions of people. We don't need to scrap it but we do need to clean it up. By thinking cautiously, creatively and with vision, it is possible to develop an industrial sector that will benefit people without jeopardising the planet.

Clean Production

The aim of 'clean production' is to enable us to fulfil our need for industrial production sustainably. It is a holistic concept (takes account of the whole, not just selected parts) which involves more than just recycling, or using renewable resources. As well as designing things to be refilled and repaired, or selecting non-toxic, degradable materials with which to make them, a clean production approach questions the need for every product and requires thought and creativity to design and produce the things that we do need in an environmentally (and socially) benign way. The theory of clean production has already been developed and the practice of it is emerging as I write. The theory rests on these three principles:

1. The Preventative Approach

This requires forethought. Preventing waste is cheaper and safer than dealing with it. Redesigning products and processes can eliminate useless solid waste and toxic by-products. For example:

- Phasing out PVC plastic (which has already started in some countries) eliminates pollution during manufacture and at disposal. When incinerated, PVC is responsible for creating extremely poisonous dioxins because it contains chlorine. Nike are blazing a trail by phasing out the use of PVC in their trainers.
- Multifunction goods use less resources and take up less space. A common example is the telephone/answer machine or the washing machine/tumble dryer. We are also beginning to see photocopier/fax/scanner machines, integrated television and videos and multifunction power tools. Watch out for further development of multifunction goods in the future.

2. The Precautionary Approach

This reverses the burden of proof by requiring the potential polluter to prove that products and processes are safe, rather than society having to prove otherwise. Environmental groups in the UK and Europe are starting a new campaign for chemicals to be shown to be safe before approval by government, rather than having to be proved harmful as at present. A new coalition of groups has formed to work towards this end. It includes Friends of the Earth, The World Wide Fund for Nature (WWF), Greenpeace and the Women's Environmental Network.

3. Real Democracy

Employees, consumers and local communities are all affected by industrial processes. It seems only fair that all these people have easy access to information about industrial practices and pollution track records as well as involvement in the decision-making process. In the United States, the Freedom of Information Act is a step towards real democracy. Similar, though weaker legislation has been proposed for the UK – it can only be a good thing.

Priorities for clean production
- the use of renewable, non-hazardous resources
- the use of minimum resources for maximum advantage
- the longest life possible
- recyclability of materials
- easy disassembly for repair or ultimately recycling
- safe degradability where recycling is not possible.

The principles of clean production have been the inspiration for the development and use of many materials and products which minimise our impact on the Earth. But sustainable development requires all production to be clean production. Clean industry needs to be the rule rather than the exception.

What You Can Do

- Use your voice as a consumer and a citizen to express your support for clean production. Use your purchasing power with care (seek advice if you need it) and use your pen power frequently! Write to the prime minister, your MP, anybody you consider relevant and ask why the government isn't taking more action to clean up industry. Talk about clean production and your desire to reduce waste.
- If you live near an industrial area you might choose one company to approach and enquire about their waste output. You might be pleasantly surprised, or you might be able to persuade them to have an environmental audit, or donate to a scrap club. If you get good results contact your local newspaper and tell them. Your actions could be an inspiration to others!

Green Design

Being a holistic concept, clean production is not simply about industrial processes, it is about finding new and creative solutions at the design stage. We are only limited by our imagination. A document called 'Way Beyond', published by the United Nations Environment Programme (UNEP) Working Group on Sustainable Product Development features many amazing new ideas for sustainable products and processes. For example, have you ever thought of growing products? – and I don't mean food. Techniques for growing products directly are being investigated, cutting out the need for manufacture altogether. This certainly requires a leap of the imagination!

An American researcher and business woman, Dr Sally Fox, grows coloured cotton, a development from native African strains of coloured cotton plants. This eliminates the need for dyeing (a notoriously polluting process) and celebrates the existence of natural diversity.

In Holland artist Reiner Lagendijk has grown a table by guiding the roots of a growing fig tree into a table shaped mould. Designer Jan Velthuizen has employed a similar technique growing gourds into textured and shaped moulds. Gourds are fruits of the cucumber family like squashes. When they have finished growing, the gourds are dried, the seeds are taken out, and they can then be used as containers.

Other designers have been investigating the use of organic waste products as raw materials. In the US Dan Cramer has used ground corn stalks to make bowls. Alberto Lievore has used almond shells as a base product, crushed and mixed them with natural and synthetic resins to make a paste which is then heated and pressed into a mould to make the desired product, for example a chair. The resulting material is called 'Maderon' and combines many of the benefits of a wood product with the advantages of plastics manufacturing (eg using moulds means fast, low waste production). The almond shells are available annually and can be 'harvested' at no extra financial or environmental cost because they are a by-product which would otherwise go to waste.

Trevor Baylis is an increasingly familiar name in Britain. He invented the wind-up radio with people power in mind. The original model was designed for use in places in Africa where there is no electricity supply. The radio requires no batteries or mains electricity – it is simply powered by winding. The simplicity and effectiveness of this design has been popular and now a variety of 'Freeplay' radios are widely available in Britain.

> **Not just a wind-up!**
> No, the latest refinement of the Freeplay radio isn't just a wind-up. It incorporates a rechargeable battery which charges from a solar panel or the wind-up handle. This means it can store up to 14 hours worth of energy so you won't need to crank it up when it runs out in the middle of your favourite song! This latest model is really neat and compact and comes in a range of transparent plastic colours so you can see the inner workings. It costs just under £60 but it will never cost you a penny in electricity!

Trevor Baylis has also developed a wind-up torch using the same technology. I wonder what's next?! Visit the website www.freeplay.net

Bicycles work on the same principle of non-polluting human power. Bikes have been around for over a hundred years and although we've come a long way since the penny-farthing, the principle remains the same – and it's brilliant. Unfortunately in Britain we're heading for what has been described as 'Carmageddon'. Road-traffic accidents, traffic jams, road rage, pollution and depletion of resources are all realities that are on the increase. The reasons for the explosion in car ownership are complex and there is no single solution to reverse the trend. It would help if more people swapped their cars for bikes, but the increase in car traffic has made cycling more dangerous. There are groups promoting cleaner, greener transportation, like Transport 2000 that promote bicycle riding and are working towards making it a safer option. If you have a bike, use it wherever you feel safe to.

Designing products to harness solar power instead of relying on batteries or mains electricity is another green option. Batteries pose a particular problem in that they contain highly polluting chemicals which don't get recycled. They are toxic waste and aren't supposed to go to landfill. (Not many people know that – don't put them in the bin!)

You won't need any batteries with the solar powered torch! A solar panel in the handle charges an internal rechargeable battery in just a few hours when directed towards sunlight. If you keep it on a window sill it will always be topped up and ready for action. It doesn't need expensive and polluting batteries and offers really efficient energy use.

If you have a walkman or discman that you feed standard batteries, it's time for a change. Not only can you purchase some extremely long lasting rechargeable batteries, you could invest in a solar-powered battery charger. Both batteries and charger will pay for themselves by saving you forking out on one-use batteries or mains electricity (for a plug-in charger). You can use these money saving arguments to negotiate with your parents!

So where are these groovy green products?
You can't always find new and innovative products in high street shops – it can take a while for novel ideas to hit the mainstream. So check out the Shopping part of the Resources section at the back of this book. Ring up the Centre for Alternative Technology and Natural

> Collection for their mail-order catalogues. Show your friends and family. Supporting good new inventions will bring them into the mainstream and make them easier for everyone to find. Just a couple of years ago the wind-up radio was totally obscure, now you can find them in high street stores.

What you can do
- Get inventing! Redesign a wasteful product!
- Choose green design wherever you have the option.
- If you buy green and you like it spread the word. Me, I love my wind-up radio!

Take back policies

Businesses small and large are beginning to take on board their legal obligations regarding producer responsibility. They are finding ways of reducing the waste they produce. This is often begun by concerned individuals in a few companies, and this blazes a trail for others to follow.

You can do your bit by supporting companies that have take-back policies and spreading the word to others. Ink Again printer cartridges are sold with a freepost envelope so that you can return your empty cartridge for recycling. In addition, they donate at least 50p per cartridge to Tommy's Campaign which funds research into miscarriage, premature birth and still birth. If you have a printer at home look out for Ink Again.

Rank Xerox are famous for their photocopy machines. They now have what is called the zero landfill machine. It's guaranteed to be repaired and recycled, and not to end up in a muddy grave. This is exactly the response we need from industry. If Xerox can do it, what's stopping everyone else from copying?!

If your household is thinking of buying a computer, a TV, or similar piece of equipment why not write a few letters to different manufacturers and explain that you want to buy from a company that has a take-back policy. Let the companies know you have a conscience, if they want a stake in the future they had better listen to you because you're the next generation of (ethical) consumers!

Dematerialisation — Services Not Products

It is possible to make a big reduction in the resources we are using without the bottom falling out of our economy. 'Dematerialisation' is one way of reducing our need for resources. It's not about disappearing off into the ether! It's about using services rather than buying products.

The simplest way to explain this is by giving some examples. Using a library service means borrowing rather than buying, and one book can be read by many people. This clearly makes more efficient use of resources. Launderettes, nappy washing services and hire shops all involve the consumer buying a service rather than a product.

There are advantages in this for people and the planet. Our patterns of consumption and employment could change considerably. By supporting such services we would be supporting and generating local employment and in some places helping a sense of community to re-emerge where it has disappeared. We could see more local shopping, away from the superstore out-of-town shopping that has been impinging on high street economies and our countryside for the past decade or so. Individuals would avoid buying expensive goods and the associated responsibility of maintenance and upkeep. Homes could be less cluttered with appliances.

The idea of maximising resource efficiency must be taken on board by all sectors of society. Take our homes, for example. New homes could be designed differently to promote efficiency – eg small blocks of flats could share a utility room with washing machine, tumble dryer etc. Instead of every household needing an appliance, perhaps four households could share. This would divide purchase price and maintenance costs of appliances by four and give more space in individual homes.

In the Netherlands car-share businesses have been established. They provide a flexible system for people to use cars as and when they need them and it sounds like an excellent answer to vehicle congestion. Different schemes are run in different ways but the general principles are the same in that they are flexible, local, car-rental schemes. Once you have joined the scheme you can borrow a car when you need it, use it for as long as you like and pay for it accordingly. You are saved from the responsibilities of car ownership like paying for tax, insurance and maintenance and you are more inclined to consider the necessity of using a car because you pay for each use.

The schemes are far more flexible than standard car hire as we know it. They are designed to serve locals, so you can just walk to collect a car when you need it. Schemes like these could be instrumental in reducing traffic because they find a middle way which doesn't prevent people from using cars but encourages them to use them in a more efficient way. They would lend themselves to a rural setting as well as an urban one. Many villages suffer incredible traffic congestion as households increasingly have two cars to provide mobility (increasingly important with the decline of village services such as post offices and shops). Often there is inadequate parking space and roads fill up with stationary cars that add to congestion and safety hazards. A village car-share system could provide mobility and ease the flow of traffic.

In France, thinking along these lines has led to trial schemes where bicycles are freely available for loan in city centres. Such schemes give a new meaning to 'park and ride', which up until now has meant park your car and jump on a bus. The goal is the same – to reduce the volume of traffic in city centres. The idea is being considered in Britain. It will be interesting to see if it takes off.

In western society ownership and possession are held up as ultimate goals to achieve. But often what we actually need is just to get a job done, we don't necessarily need the product that does it for us. We need to think about the utility of things – what purpose do they serve, or what job do they do? For example, you might want to put up some bookshelves on your bedroom wall and you need a drill to make holes for the screws. Do you actually need to go and buy a drill, or do you just need to drill holes in the wall? The answer is probably the latter. Your needs could be adequately met by borrowing or hiring a drill.

You can apply the same theory to many different situations. And the idea of the *use* being more important than the *product* can link up with take-back policies. If we start to think of ourselves needing illumination rather than light bulbs then it naturally follows that when the light bulb no longer provides that illumination we'll take it back and swap it for one that does (for a price of course). Think of the product as being a channel – something through which you get light, music, visual entertainment etc. Aren't those the things we really want, not the object that conveys those things? Something to ponder over!

Dematerialisation can be used to significantly reduce the impact we make on the environment and it will work just so long as you are willing to accept the idea and take it on board. You don't have to wait for the rest of the world to do it first, be a pioneer! Everything that everyone does counts.

Changing Shopping

Chapter 2 discussed this in detail, but it didn't mention a completely different kind of shop!

Share centres

One of the obstacles preventing us from recycling more and choosing low waste products and services is the lack of easy access to such facilities. Easy access has two requirements. The first is information – you need to know where to go to deposit recyclables or get a repair done without spending ages making telephone calls and looking through telephone directories or the internet. The second requirement is locality – services need to be nearby and easy to get to so that you can take full advantage of them.

In Germany a new kind of store has been developed that allows people to be waste conscious, this is the Share centre (Second-Hand Department Store and Recycling). The centres could be described as a one-stop shop for waste prevention. The centre collects all manner of used goods, then services or repairs them where necessary and stores them for resale in the second-hand department store. The public are offered low price, good quality products which would otherwise have been regarded as rubbish. The centres provide an online computer service too which details products for sale, rent or hire. The framework of the Share centre could facilitate all sorts of waste preventing projects and services, like repair shops, community composting and laundry services. There are of course facilities to deposit recyclables too.

If everyone in Britain was living within easy reach of a facility like a Share centre, it would be so easy to change the way we shop. You could help to do that by realising your organisational potential. You don't have to rely on someone else to set up a big and complex outfit, why not organise your own? Make a plan and take it to people who can help – teachers, town clerks, mayors etc. Perhaps you can borrow a public space, like a town or village hall, on a regular basis and have an 'occasional Share centre'.

If you want to make more of a splash perhaps a one-off spectacular is your kind of thing? One such event occurred a while ago in Berkshire, it was televised for BBC1 and called *Swap Till You Drop!* The idea was very simple – anyone could bring along unwanted items and offer them in exchange for somebody else's unwanted item. All sorts of things were on offer, from children's toys to vintage cars and every imaginable thing in between.

Antiques experts were on hand to advise and inform, so it was a learning experience too. The event combined the fairly mundane activity of clearing out unwanted possessions with a day out with friends and family. The result was a great day.

A similar, but simpler event was organised in Malmesbury in Wiltshire. On Malmesbury Clear Out Day residents put their unwanted items outside their homes or at a community centre and others took what they wanted. You could contact your local recycling officer and ask for help in arranging a Clear Out Day in your town or village.

Getting your fill

We've already highlighted refill systems as a good thing, so what can we do to get more of them established? If more high-street shops were to introduce refill systems this would conserve resources and spread the word that refills are back in business. We need to persuade the business community that it has an important role to play in providing refill services. If you regularly buy a product that could be refilled, but this service isn't offered, then write to the manufacturer and ask for a refill system. Even better, if you know lots of people that agree with you, send a petition!

Denmark takes back the empties!

For over twenty years now, one trip-beer containers have been banned in Denmark. An efficient system of glass bottles with deposits, which are refilled locally, has taken their place.

Enough (the Anti-consumer Campaign) promote National No-Shop Day, an annual event aimed at making people think about their shopping habits and assessing their values. Look out for the campaign, and think about the way you shop.

Changing Advertising

Despite the 'No Junk Mail' sign on the door, plenty of adverts for pizza restaurants and taxi firms etc still plop through the letterbox. Sometimes I run down the road to hand the offending item back, but this usually makes me feel rotten because the person who made the delivery is simply trying to earn a living, and if I don't take the leaflet and recycle it it'll probably end up as litter or household waste. This got me wondering about how small businesses might advertise in a less wasteful way. I focused on the pizza restaurant and imagined an invitation to enjoy a delicious meal plopping through my letterbox. Except this time I wouldn't be in a hurry to recycle it or return to sender, because apart from it's obvious durability, the invitation offered me money back if I returned it to the restaurant. Perhaps ten pence for returning it (in person), or ten per cent off a meal if I stayed to eat. The invitation could then be used in another mail-out. Deposits on advertising! It would be interesting to see how effective this might be at boosting local business and reducing junk mail.

Celebrating Differently

Special occasions are important events in the calendar of every culture. If you don't follow an organised religion there are probably still days that are significant to you that you appreciate in a different way to other days. Celebrating is important to our well-being. It's about feeling good about ourselves and our communities. The feeling you get on a special day, and the anticipation you feel as it approaches is priceless. Growing up in the modern world, simple pleasures like the special 'feel' of a day are so easily swamped by a smog of consumerism. We're sold cards and gifts to give on an ever increasing number of occasions through the year, but are we really celebrating or just going through the motions?

Sometimes less is more. We can value more subtle ways of giving. A letter, a flower, a phone call, a home-made card. All of these things can touch our hearts and make us feel appreciated. Festivals or special occasions lose their meaning if we lose touch with what they are really about.

Christmas dominates the Christian calendar as a religious festival, but it has also become a major consumer event for the entire western world and is viewed by many as the epitome of overindulgence. There are huge pressures to buy expensive gifts for everyone you know. The pressure and expectations are so strong that the religious element is utterly overwhelmed by the shopping bonanza. If you celebrate Christmas – make it *your* festival, not the retailers'. Give it some thought and be creative! You could plan ahead and grow your own Christmas tree, one that will continue growing for many Christmases to come. Ask at a local garden centre for advice on the right type of fir tree for this. You might design and make your own decorations, make a Christmas pudding and bake a cake.

There are dozens of different festivals celebrated by

different religious groups in Britain throughout the year, but none is so apparently wasteful as Christmas. If you are aware of a wasteful dimension to your celebrations, can you think of alternatives?

> **Reusable Easter eggs!**
> Easter is another Christian festival that produces lots of waste. Fairly small chocolate eggs are presented in big cardboard boxes with a bit of plastic for good measure. You can avoid this waste by borrowing an idea from Sweden where children make and decorate a durable papier-mâché 'egg' which is brought out every year and refilled with chocolate treats!

It's good for us to consider different cultures to see how the spirit of the occasion can be retained without making so much waste. If we choose to, we can adapt our own celebrations and rituals in the light of information and inspiration from other people. We needn't shun festivals simply because we have been urged to celebrate in wasteful ways – we should reclaim the right to celebrate in meaningful ways that don't produce lots of rubbish.

Rescuing

Until such a time when waste prevention totally permeates our culture, there will always be scope for the scavengers amongst us. Skip scavenging can rescue products otherwise destined for a landfill or incinerator. It is technically illegal to take things without permission even if they have been discarded (which seems a bit odd!)

so it's advisable to ask first. Many large shops throw out huge amounts of goods which are perfectly useful. Sometimes people hire a skip when they have building work done or have a big clear-out and all sorts of useful items can be rescued from such situations.

'Bin diving' can be particularly rewarding on campsites. Some friends showed me such an extensive list of rescued items from one summer holiday that I'm sure a swapshop would be a lucrative sideline for all campsite shops! Next time you're on holiday, before you splash out on a straw mat, surfboard, windbreak, tent, barbecue, camp bed, folding chair, or picnic table, do just check the bin first!

Developing the arts from your dustbin

There are many artists working today who use discarded objects as raw materials with which to express their ideas. Often the use of recovered materials is a political statement about the way our society works. That is, a comment on how much we consume and the way that we consume it.

Joanna Rucklidge began to address the issue of waste when, as a graphic-design student, she spent time at an advertising agency. She was appalled by the unnecessary waste of materials used for the creation and presentation of designs. She went on to base all of her college projects on waste issues to highlight the fact that consumer waste is an environmental problem that people have some real control over. Joanna continues to address ecological issues in her work as a freelance artist and designer and also as a design lecturer. She makes reusable sanitary towels, vases out of old glass bottles and uses old plastic bags to make new ones – these come in both knitted and patchwork varieties!

Charles Thomas is a driftwood furniture maker and beach clearer. He uses wood and netting to make strong, robust articles. The wood has already been sculpted by the sea to give strange, interesting polished forms. A piece of furniture made in this way holds mystery and fantasy. A functional item, but a work of art too.

One exhibition at the Crafts Council in London showed work produced entirely from recycled materials. It's inspiring to know that if you have the desire to be creative you can always find raw materials to work with. Orthodox artists' materials can be so expensive!

Musical chairs!

So often, seeing rubbish and waste around can make people feel fed up and dissatisfied with their environment, and they get despondent. This wasn't the case for a bunch of young people from Plymouth, for whom rubbish was the beginning of a very creative and fun process. They have formed a band called the Weapons of Sound and I came across them when they were featured on a TV programme. Forming a band is not so unusual for a group of friends, but this band is more than a little special. All of the band members are literally playing with rubbish. They make their instruments out of things that have been thrown away, thus preventing waste and creating unique (even weird!) musical instruments. Their creations range from the relatively regular dustbins and plastic piping to the positively peculiar kitchen sink and shopping trolley! They are making amazing sounds and promoting waste prevention in a quite spectacular way and have appeared at Glastonbury and other festivals as well as the Albert Hall. Look, and listen out for them – www.soundhouse.co.uk

Campaigning

Campaigning against wasteful practices and promoting reuse solutions can be extremely effective.

Brent Spa

When the giant oil company Shell decided that their oil platform Brent Spa was redundant, they thought they would dump it in the North Sea. Greenpeace launched a protest campaign which caught the public imagination. The strength of public feeling forced the oil giant to reconsider its 'disposal' plans. After a long period of consultation it was decided that Brent Spa was not to be dumped, but reused as a quay in Norway. The transformation process is now underway.

The saga of the Brent Spa demonstrates to the big corporations that their actions are subject to public scrutiny and that the public do have a conscience that they are willing to act on. It also proves that even for such a huge project, reuse and recycling are feasible options and they need to be considered and not dismissed out of hand.

What You Can Do: Think, Care, Act, Talk

Think positive, and think big! What you do can change the world for the better. Think about the issues raised in this book. If it makes sense to you not to throw our world away then that means you already do care. Relate waste prevention to your own life and find ways of taking action. You might start in some small way as you are pondering your lifestyle and wondering where to make other changes. Don't ever feel that a small change is insignificant. It isn't, it's the way forward, especially because we're talking about lifestyle changes not just about changing the brand of shampoo you use. Shampoo may well be part of it(!) but the real positive impact comes when people make lasting changes because they have undergone a change in perception. If you stop thinking of 'waste' and start thinking of 'resources' then you have undergone that transformation! As a convert to the zero waste future you can spread the word to others and set a positive example to inspire others.

- You can support environmental campaigns by becoming a member of a group or organisation and by getting more informed. Joining with like-minded people can be very inspiring and it gives weight to the campaign because the bigger the body of support for an issue, the more seriously industry and the government will take it. Contact the Women's Environmental Network for details of campaigns, projects, information briefings and how to join. See Resources for other organisations to get involved with.
- You could set up a waste minimisation project at your school, college and/or workplace.
- If you see the need to set up a campaign in your area, you can learn a lot from existing campaign groups. You need to know your facts, so get reading and talking. You'll need an action plan with ideas of how to raise awareness about your campaign issue. You can talk to the press (and they love photo opportunities), hold a public meeting, produce information leaflets for distribution, organise a petition addressed to the relevant organisation/person involved (for example, a

government minister or director of a company). Most of all you'll need plenty of energy and enthusiasm, and the support of a few committed friends is worth its weight in gold.

- You may not be quite ready to take on the might of big business and the bureaucracy of government, but there is still loads you can do to make a difference. You can practice your campaigning skills on your family and friends. Can you inspire them to make changes? Can you convince them that it makes sense? Bear in mind that time-saving, money-saving changes will usually be most welcome!
- As a curious and provocative being you can ask questions and ask individuals, companies and governments to account for their actions and inactions. Form your opinion and then voice it. Send letters and petitions wherever you think it appropriate. Your opinion counts, so let it be heard.
- Use this book as a springboard into the environmental movement. Your energy, enthusiasm, creativity and concern for the planet will change the world. You don't have to be living in a tree or holed up in a tunnel to be an eco-warrior building a sustainable future! Whatever path you travel in life, if you carry with you respect for the planet and its resources you will be making a difference.
- We are more likely to achieve the goals of sustainable development by working with the business and industrial community rather than against them. We can identify wasteful processes and products and rather than try to eliminate them we can think about the purpose they serve and set about designing a less

wasteful alternative. Design should be the growth industry of the new century!

The Way Ahead

Human development has largely caused our environmental problems but human activity can equally well rise to the challenge of protecting the planet so that future generations of humans and all other species can flourish.

Although we need to make changes, we mustn't be ecological martyrs, the changes must be life-enhancing, not depriving. Making gradual, permanent adjustments to our lives is likely to be more effective than trying to go beyond the bin overnight and finding it impossible to keep up the initial enthusiasm. We can take encouragement, advice and inspiration from other societies, groups and individuals who are shining examples of all the weird and wonderful ways in which we can tread a little less heavily on this planet.

50 Tips For Action

1. Take a lunch box full of goodies and avoid plastic-packed sandwiches.
2. Take your own shopping bag or rucksack when you go shopping and cut down the carrier-bag mountain.
3. Try solid shampoo – it doesn't need a bottle and its compact size makes transportation more efficient and less polluting.
4. Start composting your kitchen waste.
5. Grow some flowers – don't buy cut flowers wrapped in cellophane.
6. Try a deodorant crystal instead of roll-on or spray (see Natural Collection catalogue).
7. Be inventive when it comes to present giving. If you don't know what to buy, why not give your time rather than your money? You could cook a meal or run an errand, or tidy up! These things don't come

gift-wrapped, but if you explain what you want to do and why, they're bound to be appreciated.
8. Choose a soft drink in a can or bottle that can be recycled, rather than a carton that can't.
9. Even better, use a cafe with real cups and glasses where you can sit down and have a rest as well as a drink.
10. Do your bit – do the recycling trip!
11. Wherever you feel safe to do so, walk or use a bike for short journeys.
12. If you don't already use a milkround, ask your parents to start. Point out the reasons why and offer to arrange it for them if they're too busy.
13. Do the same with a vegetable-box scheme. Find out from the Soil Association where your local box scheme operates. If it's close enough for you to use, sell the idea to your parents.
14. Make your own popcorn to take to the cinema in a compostable bag or reusable container! It's great fun, really cheap, tastes great and saves the litter and waste of empty cartons.
15. Have a clothes clear-out with some friends – you could swap things you're bored with and have an alternative fashion parade into the bargain.
16. Mend something that has broken!
17. Use rechargeable batteries.
18. Invest in a solar powered battery charger. Put the case to your parents that this would pay for itself and benefit the environment. Work out how much money it could save over a year.
19. Buy recycled.
20. If possible, send e-mails instead of letters.
21. Share a magazine with a friend, or read it at the

library if they have it.
22. Save envelopes and Jiffy bags. Buy envelope re-users (contact WEN) or plain labels (recycled) to make your old envelopes function again.
23. If you don't have them already, campaign for low energy light bulbs in your house! They use less than a quarter of the electricity of conventional light bulbs and last about ten times as long. Lower electricity bills are bound to impress the bill payers!
24. Set up a paper recycling scheme at school or college.
25. Talk to people about waste saving activities and why it's the way to go.
26. Visit the Centre for Alternative Technology.
27. Try reusable sanitary protection.
28. Cook some friends a meal instead of going out for fast food.
29. Think of the bin as a no-go zone!
30. Buy a toothbrush with a replacable head from the Natural Collection catalogue.
31. Buy one for a friend too.
32. Talk to your headteacher about Book Aid. Perhaps your school has suitable books it can donate.
33. Use a solar powered calculator. These are readily available and have been used for years!
34. Check out the Weapons of Sound website www.soundhouse.co.uk and go to a gig if there's one near you.
35. Visit the Earth Centre.
36. Order a copy of the Natural Collection catalogue for someone else.
37. Stop the junk mail falling through your letterbox by contacting the Mailing Preference Service, Freepost

22, London W1E 7EZ. Contact the Royal Mail about unaddressed items that are delivered by your postie. Could this be the perfect birthday present for the parent who has everything?!

38. If your parents are clearing out a garden shed or garage and unearth some unwanted or broken tools, contact Tools for Self-Reliance who will mend and export them to developing countries.
39. Visit a charity shop or jumble sale.
40. Write to a supermarket or two (addresses on own-brand products) and enquire about over packaged goods. My pet hate is instant coffee in glass jars. Why don't they do refill packs in foil or paper?
41. Write letters of complaint wherever you spot a gross waste of resources.
42. Consider the quality of the new clothes that you buy. Well made clothes may cost more but they should last much longer.
43. If you have any doubt as to whether something can be recycled or reclaimed in some way then contact your local recycling officer for advice and information.
44. Borrow something instead of buying. And always return borrowed things promptly – people are usually happy to lend so long as you are respectful and careful.
45. If your family likes yoghurt, make some at home and avoid all those plastic pots.
46. Do a waste audit for yourself or your family. Formulate a plan of how you can reduce waste and then act on it. Get the whole household involved. Make targets and schedule in (low waste!) treats for reaching the targets!

47. Avoid all the packaging, bake a loaf of bread!
48. Think about activities and businesses that don't cause waste or provide alternatives to wasteful products, and encourage and support them.
49. Check out some more green books!
50. And most importantly, enjoy doing all of the above!

Resources

Information

'Are you doing your bit?' Campaign
Tel 0345 868 686
www.doingyourbit.org.uk
Ideas for people to protect and improve the planet from the Department of Environment, Transport and the Regions.

BioRegional Development Group
Sutton Ecology Centre
Honeywood Walk
Carshalton
Surrey SM5 3NX
Tel 020 8773 2376
www.bioregional.com
Information on local production of recycled paper and much more.

Black Environment Network
9 Llainwen
U Chaf
Llanberis
Wales LL55 4LL
Tel 01286 870 715
Works to enable full ethnic participation in sustainable development.

Centre for Alternative Technology
Llwyngwern Quarry
Machynlleth
Powys SY20 9AZ
Tel 01654 702 400
help@catinfo.demon.co.uk
www.cat.org.uk
Mail order catalogue – Buy Green By Mail;
visitor and information centre.

Community Composting Network
Dave Middlemass
67 Alexandra Road
Sheffield S2 3EE
A membership organisation producing a quarterly magazine and providing information and advice on community composting.

Composting Association
Ryton Organic Gardens
Coventry CV8 3LG
Tel 01203 303517
www.compost.org.uk
Information on composting.

Council for Environmental Education
94 London Street
Reading
Berkshire RG1 4SJ
Tel 01189 502 550
Promotes environmental education, has publications and a resource library.

Council for the Protection of Rural England (CPRE)
Warwick House
25 Buckingham Palace Road
London SW1W 0PP
Tel 020 7976 6433
info@cpre.org.uk
www.greenchannel.com/cpre
Works to protect and enhance our countryside.

The Earth Centre
Denaby Main
Doncaster DN12 4EA
Tel 01709 513 933
info@earthcentre.org.uk
www.earthcentre.org.uk
A theme park, museum, science experiment all rolled into one.

Enough (Anti-Consumer Campaign)
One World Centre
6 Mount Street
Manchester M2 5NS
Tel 0161 226 6668
www.enviroweb.org/enviroissues/enough

Friends of the Earth (England, Wales & Northern Ireland)
Underwood Street
London N1 7JQ

Tel 020 7490 1555
info@foe.co.uk
www.foe.co.uk
Environmental pressure group
and membership organisation.

**Friends of the Earth Ireland
(Earthwatch)**
20 Grove Road
Rathmines
Dublin 6
Tel 00 35 1 497 3773
foeeire@iol.ie

**Friends of the Earth
Scotland**
Bonnington Mill
72 Newhaven Road
Edinburgh EH6 5QG
Tel 0131 554 9977
foescotland@gn.apc.org
www.foescotland.org

Greenpeace UK
Greenpeace House
Canonbury Villas
London N1 2PN
Tel 020 7865 8100
editor@uk.greenpeace.org
www.greenpeace.org.uk
Environmental pressure group
and membership organisation.

**Henry Doubleday
Reasearch Association
(HDRA)**
Ryton Organic Gardens
Coventry CV8 3LG
Tel 01203 303 517
enquiry@hdra.org.uk
www.hdra.org.uk
Information on composting
and organic gardening.

**Marine Conservation
Society**
9 Gloucester Road
Ross-on-Wye
Herefordshire HR9 5BU
Tel 01989 566 017
Produces information and
campaigns to conserve the
marine environment. Organises
the annual beachwatch survey.

Minewatch
54 Camberwell Road
London SE5 0EN
Tel 020 7277 4852
minewatch@gn.apc.org
Provides information on the
impact of mining – primarily
on the environment and local
communities, especially on
indigenous peoples.

The Soil Association
Bristol House
40–56 Victoria Street
Bristol BS1 6BY
Tel 0117 929 0661
info@soilassociation.org
www.soilassociation.org
Details of organic box schemes.

Surfers Against Sewage
Old Counthouse Warehouse
Wheal Kitty
St Agnes
Cornwall TR5 0RE
Tel 0845 4583001
www.sas.org.uk
Single-issue pressure group working to improve the beach environment.

Tidy Britain Group
The Pier
Wigan
Lincs WN3 4EX
Tel 01942 824 620
www.tidybritain.org.uk
Provides information on waste and litter.

Transport 2000
The Impact Centre
12–18 Hoxton Street
London N1 6NG
Tel 020 7613 0743
transport2000@transport2000.demon.co.uk
Campaigns for sustainable transport.

Waste Watch
Europa House
Ground Floor
13–17 Ironmonger Row
London EC1V 3OG
WasteLine 0870 243 0136
www.wastewatch.org.uk
Information on waste prevention and recycling.

Women's Environmental Network (WEN)
PO Box 30626
London E1 1TZ
Tel 020 7481 9004
wenuk@gn.apc.org
www.gn.apc.org/wen
Membership organisation campaigning and informing on environmental and health issues of particular relevance to women.

World Resource Foundation
Heath House
133 High Street
Tonbridge
Kent TN9 1DH
Tel 01732 368 333
Information on waste management and prevention.

World Wide Fund For Nature (WWF), formerly the World Wildlife Fund
Panda House
Weyside Park
Godalming
Surrey GU7 1XR
Tel 01483 426 444
www.wwf-uk.org

Wyecycle
Richard Boden

18 Scotton Street
Wye
Ashford
Kent TN25 5BZ
Tel 01233 813298
Village waste minimisation project. Information on composting kitchen and garden waste available.

Shopping
The Body Shop
Watersmead Business Park
Littlehampton
West Sussex BN17 6LS
Tel 01903 844 044
e-mail info@bodyshop.co.uk
www.the-body-shop.com
To find out about the origins, ethics and day-to-day workings of the company, Body Shop Tours are available all year round in Littlehampton. You can get a leaflet from your local Body Shop or phone for details. There is a charge, but concessions are available for under 16s, students and school groups.

Ecover Washing Line
169 New Greenham Park
Newbury
Berks RG15 8JH
Information about Ecover products.

Freeplay Energy Europe Ltd
Cirencester Business Park
Love Lane
Cirencester GL7 4AY
Tel 0800 731 3052 for stockists
www.freeplay.net
Wind-up radios and torches.

Growing Communities
The Old Fire Station
Leswin Road
London N16 7NY
Tel 020 7923 0412
grow.communities@btinternet.com
www.btinternet.com/~grow.communities
Organic box scheme and growing sites for local food production in North London.

Lush
29 High Street
Poole
Dorset BH15 1AB
Tel 01202 668 545
www.lush.co.uk
Check out the solid shampoo bars. For mail-order service, details of your nearest shop or a copy of the fab Lush newspaper.

Magpie Home Delivery
Saunders Park View Depot
Lewes Road
Brighton BN2 4AY
Tel 01273 621 222

www.magpiehomedelivery.co.uk
Local home delivery of organic food and refill service for drinks and Ecover products. Also a recycling service. Brighton and Hove area.

Natural Collection Catalogue
PO Box 2111
Bath BA1 2ZQ
Tel 01225 442 288
www.greenstore.co.uk
All sorts of environmentally friendly and waste saving goods, including hemp shampoo bars.

Neal's Yard Remedies (office)
24–34 Ingate Place
Battersea
London SW8 3NS
Tel 020 7498 1686
For mail-order catalogue and details of shops.

Organics Direct
7 Willow Street
London EC2 4BH
Tel 020 7729 2828
www.organicsdirect.co.uk
Nationwide organic home delivery service.

Out of This World (head office)
106 High Street
Gosforth
Newcastle-upon-Tyne NE23 1HB
Tel 0191 213 5377
www.ootw.ndirect.co.uk
Shops in Newcastle, Cheltenham and Nottingham offering an alternative to supermarket shopping.

PitRok Ltd
PO Box 1416
London W6 9WH
www.pitrok.co.uk
Crystal deodorant.

Reusable Sanpro Stockists:

- **Born**
64 Gloucester Road
Bishopston
Bristol BS7 8BH
Tel 0117 924 5080
born@dial.pipex.com
www.first-born.co.uk

- **The Carrying Kind**
Elspeth Campbell
123 Station Road
Wigston
Leicester LE18 2DN
Tel 0116 257 1897

- **The Keeper**
PO Box 616
Bristol BS99 5UN
www.menses.co.uk
This is a small rubber 'cup' worn internally.

- **Moontime Alternatives**
Rose Cottage
Petworth Road
Witley
Surrey GU8 5PL
Tel 01428 684 061

- **Nature's Alternatives**
PO Box 172
Preston PR2 2WI
Tel 01772 467546
naturesalternat@hotmail.com

- **River-Moon**
Gail Lovatt
67 Southfield Road
Edgbaston
Birmingham B16 0JP
Tel 0121 420 1900

Joanna Rucklidge
Tel 020 7277 4520
Makes and sells reusable sanitary towels, wine-bottle vases and knitted plastic shopping bags.

More information is available from the Women's Environmental Network. You will be able to speak to women who have tried different products to help you decide what might be best for you.

Natracare produce fully biodegradable sanpro available through a number of outlets including healthfood/wholefood shops. If your local shop doesn't supply them, ask if they will stock them for you.

Reuse
Book Aid International
39–41 Coldharbour Lane
London SE5 9NR
Tel 020 7733 3577
www.bookaid.org
Redistributes books overseas.

Business in the Community – Gifts In Kind
44 Baker Street
London W1M 1DH
Tel 020 7224 1600
www.bitc.org.uk
Helps companies to donate unwanted goods to voluntary organisations.

BytesTwice (Association of Community Computer Reuse Projects)
c/o Waste Watch
Tel 020 7253 6266

CREATE
Speke Hall Road
Speke
Liverpool L24 9HA
Tel 0151 448 1748
Community projects renovating 'white' goods (fridges, washing machines etc).

Furniture Recycling Network
c/o SOFA
Pilot House
41 King Street
Leicester LE1 6RN
Tel 0116 233 7007
Redistributes unwanted furniture.

The London Woodbank
Woodlands Farm
331 Shooters Hill
Greenwich
London SE16 3RP
Tel 020 8691 8807
Sells pre-used wood cheaply to community organisations, artists etc.

National Association of Nappy Services
Tel 0121 693 4949
To find your nearest service and info about reusables.

The Real Nappy Association
PO Box 3704
London SE26 4RX
Tel 020 8299 4519
www.realnappy.com
Send a large s.a.e. with two stamps for details of mail-order nappies and advice.

Recycle-IT
c/o SKF UK Ltd
Sundon Park Road
Luton LU3 3BL
Tel 01582 49 2436
Sells reconditioned PCs to the public. Also involved in distributing PCs for the government's pilot scheme Computers Within Reach – to supply PCs to people on low incomes. You can call 0870 000 2288 to register interest. Low cost machines are also available to students.

TAM Direct
Tel 01707 330111
Supply reconditioned PCs to the public. Call for a price list.

Tools For Self-Reliance
(National Office)
Netley Marsh
Southampton SO40 7GJ
Tel 01703 869 697
Redistributes tools overseas.

Useitagain
www.useitagain.org.uk
A new website promoting reducing, reusing and recycling.

Vision Aid Overseas
12 The Bell Centre
Newton Road
Crawley RH10 2FZ
Tel 01293 535016
www.vao.org.uk
Collects spectacles for use overseas.

Weapons of Sound
wos@soundhouse.co.uk
www.soundhouse.co.uk
Making music out of rubbish.

Recycling

Aluminium Can Recycling (ALCAN)
PO Box 108
Latchford Locks Office
Warrington
Cheshire WA4 1NP
Freephone 0800 262 465
www.alcan.co.uk

Aluminium Can Recycling Association (ACRA)
5 Gatsby Court
176 Holliday Street
Birmingham B1 1TJ
Tel 0121 633 4656

Aluminium Foil Recycling Campaign
Bridge House
53 High Street
Bidford-on-Avon
Warwickshire B50 4BG
Tel 01789 490609
information@alufoil.co.uk
www.alufoil.co.uk

Brita Water Filters
Brita House
The Summit Centre
Hanworth Road
Sunbury-on-Thames
TW16 5BH
Return used Brita water filters for recycling.

British Glass Manufacturers Association
Northumberland Road
Sheffield
South Yorks S10 2UA
Tel 0114 268 6201
info@glass-ts.com
www.britglass.co.uk
Information and bottle-bank directory.

British Plastics Federation
4–6 Bath Place
Rivington Street
London EC2A 3JE
Tel 020 7457 5000

British Telecom
You can return old BT phones to a BT shop for recycling.

Community Recycling Network
10–12 Picton Street
Montpellier
Bristol BS6 5QA
Tel 0117 942 0142
Advice and information for recycling groups and organisations.

Crisp (Community Recycling in Southwark

Project)
Unit 3, Sumner Road
   Workshops
London SE15 6LA
Tel 020 7703 5222

Dunlop Footwear
Mr R Harrington (Recycling Dept)
Dunlop Footwear
Hazeldene Road
Liverpool L9 2BA
Tel 0151 525 1619
Send your old PVC wellies for recycling.

Independent Glass Recyclers Association
c/o Pharoah & Co
Boreham Ind. Estate
Waltham Road
Boreham
Essex CM3 3AW
Tel 01245 465 316

Independent Waste Paper Processors Association
19 High Street
Daventry
Northants NN11 4BG
Tel 01327 703 223
www.iwppa.co.uk
Free booklet.

Industry Council for Electronic Recycling (ICER)
6 Bath Place
London EC2A 3JE
Tel 020 7729 4766

Ink Again
Crown House
60 North Circular Road
London NW10 0QS
Tel 020 8963 0666
Takes back their printer ink cartridges for recycling.

Mobile Phones
Alcatel, Ericsson, Motorola, Nokia and Panasonic phones and their batteries can be recycled by returning them to a BT Communication Centre or posting them back in the prepaid envelope supplied at the close of your contract.

Oxfam
274 Banbury Road
Oxford OX2 7DZ
Tel 01865 311 311
oxfam@oxfam.org.uk
www.oxfam.org.uk

Paper Focus magazine
Church House
Church Lane
Kings Langley
Herts WD4 8JP
Tel 01923 261 555
Guide to recycled printing and writing papers.

Pulp & Paper Information Centre
Papermakers House
1 Rivenhall Road
Westlea
Swindon
Wiltshire SN5 7BD
Tel 0906 680 0035 (calls charged at 25p a minute)
ppic@paper.org.uk
www.ppic.org.uk

RECOUP
9 Metro Centre
Welbeck Way
Shrewsbury Avenue
Woodstone
Peterborough
Tel 01733 390 021
www.recoup.org
Promotes recycling of plastic bottles and collection schemes.

Save-A-Cup Recycling Co. Ltd
Suite 2
Bridge House
Bridge Street
High Wycombe
Bucks HP11 2EL
Tel 01494 510 167
saveacup@btclick.com
www.save-a-cup.co.uk

Steel Can Recycling Information Bureau
69 Monmouth Street
London WC2H 9DG
Tel 020 7379 1306
www.scrib.org

Textile Recycling Association
PO Box 124
Huntingdon
Cambridgeshire PE18 7DP
Tel 01954 268000
Free booklet available.

Other useful addresses
Advertising Standards Authority
2 Torrington Place
London WC1E 7HW
Tel 020 7580 5555
www.asa.org.uk
Contact the ASA if you have a complaint about any advert you have seen or heard.

Department of the Environment, Transport and Regions
Waste Strategy Division
Ashdown House
123 Victoria Street
London SW1E 6DE
Tel 020 7944 6408
wastestrategy@detr.gov.uk
www.detr.gov.uk/waste strategy

The Environment Agency
Head Office
Rio House

Waterside Drive
Aztec West
Almondsbury
Bristol BS12 4UD
Tel 0645 333 111
The agency is responsible for the protection of the environment (including waste regulation) in England and Wales. Call this general enquiry line for details of your local Environment Agency Office.

Environmental Hotline
Tel 0800 80 7060
24-hour emergency hotline for reporting all environmental incidents relating to air, land and water in England, Wales and Scotland.

Mailing Preference Service
Freepost 22
London W1E 7EZ
Tel 020 7766 4410
Apply to have your name removed from mailing lists.

Your MP
If you don't know who your local MP is you can ask at a local library. Once you know, you can write to her/him directly at:
House of Commons
London SW1A 0AA

The Prime Minister
10 Downing Street
London SW1A 2AA
Tel 020 7930 4433

Your recycling officer
Listed under local council in the phone book.
Your library may have info. produced by your recycling officer.

Scottish Environmental Protection Agency (SEPA)
Head Office
Erskine Court
Castle Business Park
Stirling FK9 4TR
Tel 01786 457700
info@sepa.org.uk
www.sepa.org.uk
SEPA is responsible for the protection of the environment (including waste regulation) in Scotland.

Silver Moon Women's Bookshop
68 Charing Cross Road
London WC2H 0BB
Tel 020 7836 7906
Great bookshop, check it out if you can.

grab a Livewire!
real life, real issues, real books, real bite

Rebellion, rows, love and sex . . . pushy boyfriends, fussy parents, infuriating brothers and pests of sisters . . . body image, trust, fear and hope . . . homelessness, bereavement, friends and foes . . . raves and parties, teachers and bullies . . . identity, culture clash, tension and fun . . . abuse, alcoholism, cults and survival . . . fat thighs, hairy legs, hassle and angst . . . music, black issues, media and politics . . . animal rights, environment, veggies and travel . . . taking risks, standing up, shouting loud and breaking out . . .

. . . grab a Livewire!

For a free copy of our latest catalogue,
send a stamped addressed envelope to:

The Sales Department
Livewire Books
The Women's Press Ltd
34 Great Sutton Street
London EC1V 0LQ
Tel: 020 7251 3007
Fax: 020 7608 1938

Juliet Gellatley
The Livewire Guide to Going, Being and Staying Veggie!

So vegetarians are unhealthy? Worn out from spending all that time cooking complex dinners? Stupidly caring about animals while children suffer? RUBBISH!!!

Juliet Gellatley looks at how farm animals are kept – at live export, slaughter, fish farming, environmental destruction and diseases in meat.

But this superb, definitive book also shows how being veggie is more healthy and could feed the whole world. It gives tips for virgin veggies and suggests ways of dealing with hassle from parents, teachers, friends and enemies – with answers to the 40 most irritating questions you're bound to be asked!

Juliet Gellatley is the Director of Viva! and winner of the first Linda McCartney Award for Animal Welfare.

'Impassioned and comprehensive' *Books for Keeps*

'A useful and informative guide' *Good Housekeeping*

Non-Fiction £4.99
ISBN 0 7043 4939 6

Caroline Clayton
Dirty Planet
The Friends of the Earth Guide to Pollution

**'Takes the mystery out of saving the planet.
Read this book and change the world!'**
Jimy Mistry, *EastEnders*, *East is East*

Car bans in Mexico City. Oxygen Bars in Beijing. Genetically modified 'Frankenstein' food almost everywhere. *Dirty Planet* gives you the lowdown on the most pressing pollution problems and tells you exactly who is to blame – industry and governments around the world.

But don't despair! You can make a real difference with the big clean-up, and *Dirty Planet* tells you how. Featuring accounts of work young women have done to help save the planet – from working with Surfers Against Sewage in Cornwall to creating a bullfrog sanctuary in South Africa – and packed with easy, practical tips to make your home, school and neighbourhood more green and influence your local council and government, *Dirty Planet* is the book you need to make the Earth a better place.

'This excellent and straightforwardly written paperback is exactly what the subtitle proclaims it to be. In a *tour de force* of practical research and frill-free reportage, Clayton pulls together a spectacular collection of pollution facts and shows us how we can help to reverse the globe-choking spiral that they represent . . . upbeat, optimistic and above all practical' *Books for Keeps*

Non-Fiction £4.99
ISBN 0 7043 4964 7

Juliet Gellatley
Born to be Wild
The Livewire Guide to Saving Animals

'Anyone who loves animals will cheer this book out loud – and so would the animals if they could!'
Sir Paul McCartney

Sick of seeing pictures of rabbits being force-fed chemicals and kittens being smeared with weed killer? Want to do something about it? Then start right here.

Juliet Gellatley takes you on a mind-exploding journey around the world of animal cruelty. Hunting and fishing, farming and fur, zoos and circuses – there are an infinite number of ways in which humans abuse animals, for pleasure and profit.

But Juliet also offers an action plan for the great fight back. Consumer power, protests, lobbying and letter writing – it's all here with practical examples.

This passionate and practical book, by the winner of the first Linda McCartney Award for Animal Welfare and founder of Viva!, is your essential guide to saving animals – before it's too late.

'A must read! Find out what's wrong in the animal world and how we can take action'
PETA (People for the Ethical Treatment of Animals)

Non-Fiction £5.99
ISBN 0 7043 4969 8